Android Software Internals Quick Reference

A Field Manual and Security Reference Guide to Java-based Android Components

James Stevenson

Apress®

Android Software Internals Quick Reference: A Field Manual and Security Reference Guide to Java-based Android Components

James Stevenson
London, UK

ISBN-13 (pbk): 978-1-4842-6913-8
https://doi.org/10.1007/978-1-4842-6914-5

ISBN-13 (electronic): 978-1-4842-6914-5

Managing Director, Apress Media LLC: Welmoed Spahr
Acquisitions Editor: Steve Anglin
Development Editor: Matthew Moodie
Coordinating Editor: Mark Powers

Cover designed by eStudioCalamar

Cover image by Brian McGowan on Unsplash (www.unsplash.com)

Distributed to the book trade worldwide by Apress Media, LLC, 1 New York Plaza, New York, NY 10004, U.S.A. Phone 1-800-SPRINGER, fax (201) 348-4505, e-mail orders-ny@ springer-sbm.com, or visit www.springeronline.com. Apress Media, LLC is a California LLC and the sole member (owner) is Springer Science + Business Media Finance Inc (SSBM Finance Inc). SSBM Finance Inc is a **Delaware** corporation.

For information on translations, please e-mail booktranslations@springernature.com; for reprint, paperback, or audio rights, please e-mail bookpermissions@springernature.com.

Apress titles may be purchased in bulk for academic, corporate, or promotional use. eBook versions and licenses are also available for most titles. For more information, reference our Print and eBook Bulk Sales web page at http://www.apress.com/bulk-sales.

Any source code or other supplementary material referenced by the author in this book is available to readers on GitHub via the book's product page, located at www.apress.com/ 9781484269138. For more detailed information, please visit http://www.apress.com/ source-code.

Printed on acid-free paper

Table of Contents

About the Author

 **James Stevenson** has been working in the programming and computer security industry for over 4 years, and for most of that has been working as an Android software engineer. Prior to this, James graduated with a BSc in computer security in 2017.

James has featured articles on both personal websites and industry platforms such as *Infosecurity Magazine* - covering topics from security principles to android programming and security to cyber terrorism.

At the time of writing, James is a full-time security researcher, part-time PhD student, and occasional conference speaker. Outside of Android internals, James' research has also focused on offender profiling and cybercrime detection capabilities. For more information and contact details, visit `https://JamesStevenson.me`.

About the Technical Reviewer

Peter Späth Graduated in 2002 as a physicist and soon afterward became an IT consultant, mainly for Java-related projects. In 2016 he decided to concentrate on writing books on various subjects, with a primary focus on software development. With a wealth of experience in Java-related languages, the release of Kotlin for building Android apps made him enthusiastic about writing books for Kotlin development in the Android environment.

CHAPTER 1

Introduction

In 2016 there were more than five million Android developers worldwide. Three years later, in 2019, there were 2.5 billion Android devices in circulation across the world. There is no doubt that Android is a massively adopted operating system, and not going anywhere anytime soon.

This book has been designed for Android software engineers new and old, with a focus away from typical UI design. This book instead focuses on the parts of Java and the Android system that typically go forgotten when learning to build applications. This book will serve as a reference guide for techniques from device and user unique identifiers to ProGuard obfuscation to long-running services - in turn digging into some of the principles not intrinsically obvious from the get-go.

As the name may suggest, this book won't be covering Android UI development, nor will it be covering low-level C, or Kernel techniques. Instead, this book will be focusing on easily digestible, useful, and interesting techniques in Java and the Android system.

What Is This Book

- An Android Java programming reference guide for non-UI elements.

- This book covers the Android operating system from Android 4.4 to 11.0.

© James Stevenson 2021
J. Stevenson, *Android Software Internals Quick Reference*,
https://doi.org/10.1007/978-1-4842-6914-5_1

What This Book Is Not

- This book doesn't include an introduction tutorial for Java; if you're looking for this, there are many other great resources out there.

- This book doesn't cover any low-level C programming, Kernel interaction, or vulnerability research.

- While one or two aspects of the Android UI may be covered in this book, it will not be a key focus.

CHAPTER 2

Android Versions

Android 1.0 was released on September 23, 2008; since then the operating system has gone through countless changes. Table 2-1 denotes the different versions of Android (starting from version 1.5 Cupcake).

The API level in Android defines the supported API functionality on that device. If using a device's shell prompt (e.g., via the command `adb shell`, which is available as part of the Android platform tools), you can return the system property that relates to the current API level by running `getprop | grep sdk`. This can also be done via adb (Android Debug Bridge) from a connected machine.

The following shows an example output of this command as run on a Google Pixel 4a running Android 11:

```
[ro.build.version.min_supported_target_sdk]: [23]
[ro.build.version.preview_sdk]: [0]
[ro.build.version.preview_sdk_fingerprint]: [REL]
[ro.build.version.sdk]: [30]
[ro.product.build.version.sdk]: [30]
[ro.qti.sdk.sensors.gestures]: [false]
[ro.system.build.version.sdk]: [30]
[ro.system_ext.build.version.sdk]: [30]
[ro.vendor.build.version.sdk]: [30]
```

© James Stevenson 2021
J. Stevenson, *Android Software Internals Quick Reference*,
https://doi.org/10.1007/978-1-4842-6914-5_2

Table 2-1. *Android Release Versions*

Version	Codename	API Level	Release Date	Linux Kernel Version
1.5	**Cupcake**	**3**	**April 2009**	**2.6.27**
1.6	**Donut**	**4**	**September 2009**	**2.6.29**
2.0	**Eclair**	**5**	**October 2009**	**2.6.29**
2.0.1	Eclair	6		
2.1	Eclair	7		
2.2.x	**Froyo**	**8**	**May 2010**	**2.6.32**
2.3 -> 2.3.2	**Gingerbread**	**9**	**December 2010**	**2.6.35**
2.3.3 -> 2.3.7	Gingerbread	10		
3.0	**Honeycomb**	**11**	**February 2011**	**2.6.36**
3.1	Honeycomb	12		
3.2.x	Honeycomb	13		
4.0.1 -> 4.0.2	**Ice Cream Sandwich**	**14**	**October 2011**	**3.0.1**
4.0.3 -> 4.0.4	Ice Cream Sandwich	15	..	..
4.1.x	**Jelly Bean**	**16**	**July 2012**	**3.0.31**
4.2.x	Jelly Bean	17		3.4.0
4.3.x	Jelly Bean	18		3.4.39
4.4 -> 4.4.4	**KitKat**	**19**	**October 2013**	**3.10**
5.0	**Lollipop**	**21**	**June 2014**	**3.16.1**
5.1	Lollipop	22		

(*continued*)

Table 2-1. (*continued*)

Version	Codename	API Level	Release Date	Linux Kernel Version
6.0	Marshmallow	23	October 2015	3.18.10
7.0	Nougat	24	August 2016	3.18.48/4.4.0
7.1	Nougat	25		
8.0.0	Oreo	26	August 2017	3.18.72/4.4.83/4.9.44
8.1.0	Oreo	27		3.18.70/4.4.88/4.9.56
9	Pie	28	August 2018	4.4.146/4.9.118/4.14.61
10	Android 10 (Q)	29	September 2019	4.9.191/4.14.142/4.19.71
11	Android 11 (R)	30	September 2020	4.14.y/4.19.y/5.4.y

CHAPTER 3

Fundamentals

Android Sandbox

Android runs under a multiuser Linux system which means that each application, and its storage, runs under a separate user. This means that under normal circumstances, applications cannot read another application's data or internal storage. Each process uses its own virtual machine (VM) which segregates applications. Prior to API level 21 (Android 5), this would have been a Dalvik Virtual Machine, and in later versions will instead use the Android Runtime (ART). Both operate in similar fashions, where they simulate a device's CPUs, registers, and other features while running an application's compiled Dalvik bytecode. ART, however, is considered to have many performance improvements.

In these VMs applications only have access to the components that they require to run (a policy of least privilege). These individual process VMs are created by Zygote[1] (zai·gowt). Zygote is launched by the Android runtime at startup, with root permissions, with the first virtual machine and all shared Java classes and resources. When a new application wants to

---

[1] "The Zygote Process - Masters on Mobile - Medium." `https://medium.com/masters-on-mobile/the-zygote-process-a5d4fc3503db`. Accessed 11 May. 2020.

© James Stevenson 2021
J. Stevenson, *Android Software Internals Quick Reference*,
https://doi.org/10.1007/978-1-4842-6914-5_3

launch, a new Zygote process is forked and the application is bound to the thread of the new process, and its code is run inside of it, nonrequired and nonrequested permissions are dropped by Zygote so that the application only possesses the necessary permissions.

Application Components

Activities

Activities are the main entry points for Android applications. Akin to a single web page, an activity is a single screen which in general will only remain running while in the foreground. While not all activities have to be visible, most standard application activities will be. An activity can be programmatically implemented by extending the `Activity` class.

Services

In general terms services are a utility in Android for providing functionality in the background while an application is not currently running in the foreground, for example, a music player, an email client polling for emails, or a maps application. The preferred technology used for tasking services has changed in Android over the years from using `Services` to using `JobSchedulers`. These will be discussed more in Chapter 10.

Broadcast Receivers

Another entry point to the application is where the system, other applications, and the application itself can "broadcast" events that the application then receives. Broadcast receivers have restricted functionality (where, as a general rule, they can only run for 10 seconds before being considered as unresponsive[2]) and, because of this, will normally start another form of long-running service such as a foreground `Activity` or a `JobScheduler`. A broadcast receiver is implemented by extending the `BroadcastReceiver` class. These will be discussed more in Chapter 4.

Content Providers

Content providers are used to manage sets of application data so that they are sharable with other applications on a device. Using a URI other applications can query or modify the data even if the application the URI belongs to is not currently running. Examples include images, text files, SQLite databases, etc.

Manifest

An application's manifest file[3] is created precompilation and cannot be edited during runtime. These xml-like files, called `AndroidManifest.xml`, detail all of the components in a single application (activities, broadcast receivers, services, etc.). The manifest file also details permissions that the application requires, the minimum API level, as well as hardware and software features used by the application (such as a camera). While an application will only have one manifest file, imported libraries may have their own. Due to this, during the build, Gradle will merge all of these individual manifest files; the result is called a merged manifest.[4]

---

[2]"BroadcastReceiver | Android Developers." 30 Sept. 2020, `https://developer.android.com/reference/android/content/BroadcastReceiver`. Accessed 6 Dec. 2020.

[3]"Application Fundamentals | Android ...." 3 Jun. 2019, `https://developer.android.com/guide/components/fundamentals`. Accessed 11 May. 2020.

[4]"Merge multiple manifest files | Android Developers." 3 Jun. 2016, `https://developer.android.com/studio/build/manifest-merge`. Accessed 11 May. 2020.

This is evident when reversing an Android application (APK file), as (if using libraries) the reversed manifest will be significantly larger and have additional elements than the original premerged manifest.

An example of a simple AndroidManifest.xml *file can be seen here. In this example the package is called* simple_app, *it uses the* FINGERPRINT *permission (as described below), and its main entry point is an activity called* MainActivity *which has two intent filters:*

```xml
<?xml version="1.0" encoding="utf-8"?>
<manifest xmlns:android="http://schemas.android.com/apk/res/android"
    package="com.example.simple_app">

    <uses-permission android:name="android.permission.USE_FINGERPRINT" />
    <application
        android:allowBackup="true"
        android:icon="@mipmap/ic_launcher"
        android:label="@string/app_name"
        android:roundIcon="@mipmap/ic_launcher_round"
        android:supportsRtl="true"
        android:theme="@style/AppTheme">
        <activity android:name=".MainActivity">
            <intent-filter>
                <action android:name="android.intent.action.MAIN" />

                <category android:name="android.intent.category.LAUNCHER" />
            </intent-filter>
        </activity>
    </application>

</manifest>
```

Permissions

Permissions in Android follow the least privilege model where specific types of functionality are only given to applications that specifically request for them. There are two main types of permission: manifest permissions and runtime permissions (of which commonly fall into the "dangerous" permissions category). Both runtime and manifest permissions must be declared in the Android manifest; however, in addition, runtime permissions must be requested at runtime prompting the user with a dialogue (as seen in Figure 3-1) on if they are happy for the application to use the stated functionality. Runtime permissions were implemented in API level 23; however, previous to this a user will be shown all runtime permissions prior to install instead.

Figure 3-1. *Example of a runtime permission as seen by the user*

As previously stated permissions are given a permission type based on the risk they pose to users, the Android system, or other applications on a device. A summary of all permission types can be seen in Table 3-1.[5]

---

[5]"<permission> | Android Developers." 27 Dec. 2019, https://developer.android.com/guide/topics/manifest/permission-element. Accessed 8 Dec. 2020.

Table 3-1. *Permission Types*

Permission Type	Risk	Description
Normal	Low	**The default permission type**. Providing the application with isolated application-level features such as BLUETOOTH, NFC, and INTERNET.
Dangerous	High	Providing the application with access to private data or an aspect of device control such as WRITE_EXTERNAL_STORAGE, ACCESS_FINE_LOCATION, and CAMERA. Unlike the normal permission type, a runtime permission request has to be accepted by the user (at runtime via a button click) before permissions are granted by the system (or at install time on devices prior to API level 23).
Signature	Critical	This permission is only granted if the application requesting the permission is signed by the same certificate as the application that declared the permission. This is commonly used to restrict a permission type to system/preinstalled applications. These permissions normally grant either mass access to the control of the system and other applications or circumvent Android security mechanisms. This includes MANAGE_EXTERNAL_STORAGE, READ_LOGS, and CAPTURE_AUDIO_OUTPUT.

In addition to these types, additional flags can be applied to permissions including `privileged` and `development` which refer to the rights given to system and development applications, respectively.[6]

Finally there are two additional permission types that need to be considered in identifying what applications can perform what actions:

- **Hard-restricted permission** - Where a permission cannot be held by any application on the device unless the permission has been allow-listed by the installer application

- **Soft-restricted permission** - Where a permission cannot be help by any application on the device, in its full form, unless the permission has been allow-listed by the installer application

When debugging a device, permissions that would normally not be available for a standard application (such as a permission with the Signature permission type) can be granted using adb. As an example for the `READ_LOGS` permission the following command can be used to grant the permission `adb shell pm grant <Package ID> android.permission. READ_LOGS`. To retrieve an application's Package ID, see Chapter 5 or Chapter 12.

An example of a manifest permission:

```
<uses-permission android:name="android.permission. WRITE_
EXTERNAL_STORAGE "/>
```

---

[6]"R.attr | Android Developers." `https://developer.android.com/reference/android/R.attr`. Accessed 8 Dec. 2020.

An example of a runtime permission request:

```
if (Build.VERSION.SDK_INT >= 23) {
    // Notification will not be shown unless the correct
        manifest permission is set
    ActivityCompat.requestPermissions(this, new String[]
    {Manifest.permission.WRITE_EXTERNAL_STORAGE}, 1234);
}
```

At the time of writing the Android specifications,[7] list 166 different manifest permissions. Table 3-2 shows a subset of the most common of these permissions as well as their API and permission levels.

---

[7]"Manifest.permission | Android Developers." 30 Sept. 2020, `https://developer.` `android.com/reference/android/Manifest.permission`. Accessed 6 Dec. 2020.

Table 3-2. Android Permissions

Name	Permission	API Level	Description
ACCESS_COARSE_LOCATION	Dangerous	29+	Access to approximate location, via non-GPS providers (such as network provider).
ACCESS_FINE_LOCATION	Dangerous	1+	Access to a specific location, via GPS and network provider.
ACCESS_NETWORK_STATE	Normal	1+	Access to ConnectivityManager responsible for, among other things, monitoring network connection (Wi-Fi-GPRS, UMTS, etc.).
ACCESS_WIFI_STATE	Normal	1+	Access to WifiManager responsible for viewing a list of configured networks, the current active network, and results of access point scans.
ANSWER_PHONE_CALLS	Dangerous	26+	Allows the application to answer an incoming call.
BATTERY_STATS	Signature|privileged|development	1+	Allows for the aggregation of battery information and statistics.

(continued)

Table 3-2. (*continued*)

Name	Permission	API Level	Description
BLUETOOTH	Normal	1+	Allows for the pairing and connection with Bluetooth devices.
CALL_PHONE	Dangerous	1+	Allows the application to call without sending an intent to the dialer application (in turn not needing to notify the user via the UI).
CALL_PRIVILEGED	Not for use by third-party applications	1+	A less restricted version of the CALL_PHONE permission allowing the application to call any phone number including emergency numbers.
CAMERA	Dangerous	1+	Provides access to the device's cameras.
CAPTURE_AUDIO_OUTPUT	Prohibited to third-party applications	19+	Allows for nonrestricted access to record audio from the device's microphone.
CHANGE_WIFI_STATE	Normal	1+	Allows for the application to modify the device's network configuration and to connect to and disconnect from Wi-Fi access points.

Permission	Protection Level	API	Description
DELETE_PACKAGES	Prohibited to third-party applications	1+	Allows for the removal of an application. As of Android 7 user, confirmation is required if the application requesting the removal is not the same as the application that installed it.
INSTALL_PACKAGES	Prohibited to third-party applications	1+	Allows an application to install another.
INTERNET	Normal	1+	Allows an application to open network sockets.
MANAGE_EXTERNAL_STORAGE	Signature|appop|preinstalled	30+	Due to the implementation of scoped storage in Android 10 (applications having a sandboxed external storage), this permission allows for the broad managing of the external storage space.
NFC	Normal	9+	Allows for I/O operations over NFC (near-field communication).
PROCESS_OUTGOING_CALLS	Dangerous and hard restricted	1–29	Allows an application to see and redirect all outgoing calls.
READ_CONTACTS	Dangerous	1+	Allows for the reading of the user's contact information.

(continued)

Table 3-2. (*continued*)

Name	Permission	API Level	Description
READ_EXTERNAL_STORAGE	Dangerous, soft restricted	16+	Allows for an application to read from external storage. After API 19 this permission is not required to read the application's scoped storage. As of the forced implementation of scoped storage in API level 29, this only provides read only acceess.
READ_LOGS	Prohibited to third-party applications	1+	Allows for reading system log information, such as those created by DropBoxManager.
READ_PHONE_NUMBERS	Dangerous	26+	Allows for the application to read all of the device's phone numbers. By default this permission is exposed to instant applications.
READ_PHONE_STATE	Dangerous	1+	Includes the READ_PHONE_NUMBERS permission. Allows for access to device/phone information such as the current cellular network.
READ_SMS	Dangerous and hard restricted	1+	Allows for the reading of SMS messages already received by the device.

Permission	Protection level	API	Description
REBOOT	Prohibited to third-party applications	1+	Allows for the rebooting of the device.
RECEIVE_BOOT_COMPLETED	Normal	1+	Allows an application to receive the Intent. ACTION_BOOT_COMPLETED intent. This intent is broadcast after the system has finished booting.
RECEIVE_MMS	Dangerous and hard restricted	1+	Allows for an application to monitor incoming MMS messages.
RECEIVE_SMS	Dangerous and hard restricted	1+	Allows for an application to monitor incoming SMS messages.
RECORD_AUDIO	Dangerous	1+	Allows for an application to record audio.
REQUEST_DELETE_PACKAGES	Normal	26+	Allows for an application to request for either itself or another application to be deleted. This will require user interaction.
REQUEST_INSTALL_PACKAGES	Signature	23+	Allows for an application to request for the installing of an application. This will require user interaction.

(continued)

Table 3-2. (*continued*)

Name	Permission	API Level	Description
SEND_SMS	Dangerous and hard-restricted permission	1+	Allows for the sending of SMS messages.
SET_PREFERRED_ APPLICATIONS	Normal	1–15	Allows the application to modify the user's preferred (default) applications – including web browser and installer.
SET_TIME	Prohibited to third-party applications	8+	Allows for the setting of the system time.
USE_BIOMETRIC	Normal	28+	Allows for the use of device-supported hardware.
USE_FINGERPRINT	Normal	23–28	Allows for the use of device fingerprint hardware. Replaced by the USE_BIOMETRIC permission in Android API level 28.

| WAKE_LOCK | Normal | 1+ | Allows the application to initiate PowerManager Wake Locks which can prohibit the device from sleeping or from the screen dimming. |
| WRITE_EXTERNAL_STORAGE | Dangerous | 4+ | Allows for the writing to the device external storage. Also grants the READ_EXTERNAL_STORAGE permission. After API 19 this permission is not required to read/write in the application's scoped storage. As of the forced implementation of scoped storage in API level 29, this only allows for an application to read their own storage data. |

Context

Another core component in Android is Context. Colloquially referred to as the "god" class, Context[8] in Android is an interface for retrieving global information about an application's environment. It allows for accessing application-specific resources as well as application-level operations such as broadcasting, receiving intents, and launching activities. Some use cases include

- Accessing the location of the application's internal storage

- Sending a Toast or Notification dialogue

- Setting an ImageView in an activity

- Retrieving the system package manager

There are two main types of Context: an application context and an activity context. Both of these types of Context are bound to the life cycle of their respective area - where an application context is tied to the life cycle of the application and the activity context is bound to the life cycle of its activity. This means that if either is destroyed, then their respective context is garbage collected.

In addition to these two subclasses of Context, there is also ContextWrapper which can be used with the Context method getBaseContext(). Context Wrapper allows for a proxy Context to be used, where it is then possible to modify the behavior of the object without changing the original Context.

---

[8]"Context | Android Developers." https://developer.android.com/reference/android/content/Context. Accessed 11 May. 2020.

Application Context

The following returns the application context. When the application is destroyed, it will be garbage collected.

Retrieve application context:

```
getApplicationContext()
```

Activity Context

When in an `Activity` or subclass of `Activity`, use *this* to return the activity context. When the activity is destroyed, then the activity context is garbage collected.

Retrieve activity context from inside activity:

```
this
```

The Activity Life Cycle

As part of using a device, the individual activities of an application can enter many different states. The activity class provides useful callbacks that are triggered when these states are entered so that an application can respond appropriately. The full activity life cycle can be seen in Figure 3-2.

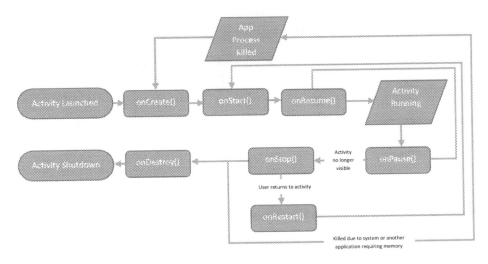

Figure 3-2. *Android application activity life cycle*

onCreate()

This callback is called when the activity is first created. This method takes a parameter of savedInstanceState which is a bundle containing the activity's previously saved state or null if it hasn't existed previously.

onStart()

This callback prepares the activity to enter the foreground and makes it visible to the user. This callback is always called each time the activity starts, unless resuming.

onResume()

When entering this state, the activity is ready to be interacted with by the user and enters the foreground. Interrupt events may occur such as a phone call or the user moving to another activity - if this occurs the activity moves to the onPause() callback.

onPause()

This callback indicates that the activity is no longer in the foreground; however, it does not necessarily mean that it is about to be destroyed.

onStop()

This callback is called before the activity is destroyed when the activity is no longer visible to the user. This is where applications should release resources. The onStop() callback is the last callback an activity will receive.

onRestart()

This activity is called after the onStop() callback when the activity is being redisplayed to the user. This is followed by onStart() and onResume().

Android Users

In Android there are two distinct concepts that could both be identified as "users".

Linux Users

Android is a multiuser Linux system where each application is sandboxed, meaning that each application is represented by a different user. The Android system assigns each unique application certificate (the certificate that the apk file is signed with) a unique Linux user ID, in turn also setting the permission of all of the application's files so that only the specified

Linux user ID can access them.[9] This means that if two applications are signed by the same certificate, then they are placed in the same sandbox. This is also required when it comes to the Signature permission type (discussed earlier) where if a permission has this type, then it can only be used by applications with the same certificate as the application that created the permission (commonly seen to prohibit nonsystem applications from accessing system permissions).

To view an application's Linux user ID, you can use adb as root to traverse to the file system of the application (e.g., /data/data/com.android. chrome) and use the ls -la command as can be seen in Figure 3-3.

```
blueline:/data/data/com.example.launcher # ls -la
total 25
drwx------    4 u0_a148 u0_a148       3488 2020-05-09 16:43 .
drwxrwx--x 201 system   system       20480 2020-05-09 16:43 ..
drwxrws--x   2 u0_a148 u0_a148_cache  3488 2020-05-09 16:43 cache
drwxrws--x   2 u0_a148 u0_a148_cache  3488 2020-05-09 16:43 code_cache
```

Figure 3-3. *Example of Linux user ID seen in the adb shell*

To view the application process ID programmatically:

```
Log.v("Application Process ID", String.valueOf(android.
os.Process.myUid()));
```

The shell command id -u can also be used via adb or via the runtime environment, as follows:

```
id -u
```

[9]"Application Signing | Android Open Source Project" 28 Oct. 2020, https:// source.android.com/devices/tech/admin/multi-user. Accessed 26 Dec. 2020.

Android Users

The second concept of users in Android is designed for multiple end users[10] of a device, designed to allow for multiple users who use the same Android device. This is achieved by having distinct application data and some unique settings per account. In turn this supports for multiple users to run in the background while another user is active.

The users currently active on a device can be found under the /data/user directory (as seen in Figure 3-4) or via the UI User screen (as seen in Figure 3-5). As different users will have their own internal and scoped storage, it is important to use the corresponding method calls (e.g., using the Context method getFilesDir()) to retrieve the correct file paths as these may change over time. A user cannot access the internal storage of another user even if it is for the same application.

```
blueline:/ $ cd /data/user
blueline:/data/user $ su
blueline:/data/user # ls
0 11
```

Figure 3-4. *Example of Android user IDs, as seen in adb shell*

---

[10]"Supporting Multiple Users | Android Open Source Project." 18 Feb. 2020, https://source.android.com/devices/tech/admin/multi-user. Accessed 11 May. 2020.

Figure 3-5. *End user's view of different users on a device*

CHAPTER 4

Intents

Intents are one of the core inter-process communication (IPC) mechanisms in Android, allowing for applications to communicate (e.g., send data or initiate an action) with other Android components (including applications) even if the recipient is not currently running. There are two main categories of intent in Android, these being:

- **Explicit** - Explicit intents are intents that specify the application or both the application and component that will action the request.

- **Implicit** - Implicit intents are more vague and specify a type of action that is desired (e.g., opening a camera or location application).

In addition to these two main categories of intents, where the message is directly sent to a specific application or service, broadcast intents can also be sent. These broadcast messages, which can be sent by the Android system or applications, are simultaneously received by all applications on the device that have previously registered for the specific broadcast action type. In some cases special permissions may be required to register for specific broadcasts (e.g., in the case of the BOOT_COMPLETE permission which allows for the receiving of an ACTION_BOOT_COMPLETED intent when the Android system finishes loading after startup).

© James Stevenson 2021
J. Stevenson, *Android Software Internals Quick Reference*,
https://doi.org/10.1007/978-1-4842-6914-5_4

Starting Components

Outside of the two categories of intent, there are three main methods for sending intents:

- **Starting an activity** - An instance of an activity can be started by passing an initialized Intent object to either the `startActivity()` or `startActivityForResult()` context methods.

- **Starting a background service** - Prior to Android 5.0 (API level 21), a background `Service` can be started by passing an initialized `Intent` object to the `startService()` context method. Post API level 21, this can be used to start `JobScheduler` components instead.

- **Sending a broadcast** - While the system sends many broadcasts at a regular frequency, such as `TIME_TICK` and `BOOT_COMPLETE`, it is also possible for an ordinary application to send its own broadcasts. In general, broadcasts are a type of intent that can be received by multiple applications simultaneously. Such a broadcast can be sent with the `sendBroadcast()` or `sendOrderedBroadcast()` context methods.

Intent Attributes

An intent comprises of several attributes. Depending on the intent being sent and the receiver, some of the following attributes may be compulsory; however, in some situations none are required. All standard intent attributes are stored as constants in the `Intent` object, for example, `Intent.FLAG_ACTIVITY_NO_HISTORY`, whose constant value is `1073741824`.

Core Attributes

- **Action** - Settable using an initialized `Intent` object's `setAction` method. The action defines the high-level action to be performed.

- **Data** - Settable using an initialized Intent object's `setData` method. The data field includes the data this intent is operating on (e.g., a file to open in an image editing app).

Additional Attributes

- **Category** - Settable using an initialized `Intent` object's `addCategory` method. Categories provide additional context about the action to be performed by the intent. Only activities that can facilitate all specified categories can be chosen to receive the intent.

- **Type** - Settable using an initialized `Intent` object's `setType` method. Normally the type is inferred from the data itself; however, this attribute can be used to set a specific MIME (Multipurpose Internet Mail Extensions) type (e.g., `audio/mpeg or audio/*`), for example, of the data to return.

- **Component** - Settable using an initialized `Intent` object's `setComponent` method. This attribute identifies the name of a component class to use for the intent. This is an optional attribute as it is normally identified based on the content of the intent.

- **Extras** - Settable using an initialized `Intent` object's `putExtra` method. An extra is a bundle (a set of key-value pairs with varying types) which the receiver can use (e.g., when sharing a note with your social media app, the note text will be sent across as a field in a bundle). This bundle can include proprietary keys or ones set in the Android system such as `EXTRA_ALARM_COUNT`.

- **Flags** - Settable using an initialized Intent object's `setFlag` method. Flags represent the behavior of the component being launched (e.g., not including the launched activity in the task stack).

Actions

Settable using an initialized `Intent` object's `setAction` method. The `getAction` method can also be used for retrieving a received intent's action. The action defines the high-level action to be performed.

An example of this can be seen here:

```
Intent intent = new Intent();
intent.setAction(Intent.ACTION_MAIN);
```

At the time of writing, the Android documentation[1] lists upward of 135 standard intent action types. Table 4-1 lists a subset of the most common intent actions.

---

[1]"Intent | Android Open Source Project." 30 Nov. 2020, `https://developer.android.com/reference/android/content/Intent#flags`. Accessed 26 Dec. 2020.

Table 4-1. Intent Actions

Name	API Level	Description
ACTION_ALL_APPS	1+	List all available applications.
ACTION_APP_ERROR	14+	Occurs when the user selects the "report" button in the crash dialogue warning message. This intent will then be sent to the installer application that installed the application that errored.
ACTION_CAMERA_BUTTON	1+	Indicating a broadcast where the device's "camera button ' has been pressed.
ACTION_CHOOSER	1+	An alternative to the default standard activity picker provided by the system. In turn this action will display an activity chooser.
ACTION_DEFAULT ACTION_VIEW	1+	A simple action which displays data to the user.
ACTION_MY_PACKAGE_ SUSPENDED	28+	A protected broadcast intent that can only be sent by the system and is sent to an application when it enters the suspended state.
ACTION_MY_PACKAGE_ UNSUSPENDED	28+	A protected broadcast intent that can only be sent by the system and is sent to an application when it leaves the suspended state.

(continued)

Table 4-1. (*continued*)

Name	API Level	Description
ACTION_PACKAGE_ ADDED	1+	A protected broadcast intent that can only be sent by the system and is sent when a new application is installed on the device, including two extras: EXTRA_UID and EXTRA_REPLACING.
ACTION_PACKAGE_ CHANGED	1+	A protected broadcast intent that can only be sent by the system and is sent when an existing application on the device has changed, including the extras: EXTRA_UID, EXTRA_CHANGED_COMPONENT_NAME_LIST, and EXTRA_DONT_KILL_APP.
ACTION_PACKAGE_ DATA_CLEARED	3+	A protected broadcast intent that can only be sent by the system and should be preceded by ACTION_PACKAGE_RESTARTED. This broadcast is sent when an application's persistent data is erased bearing in mind that this intent is not sent to the application itself, including the extras: EXTRA_UID and EXTRA_PACKAGE_NAME.
ACTION_PACKAGE_ FIRST_LAUNCH	12+	A protected broadcast intent that can only be sent by the system and is sent to the installer of an application (e.g., the Google Play Store) when an application is first launched. No extras are included; however, the data includes the name of the launched package.

ACTION_PACKAGE_RESTARTED	1+	A protected broadcast intent that can only be sent by the system and is triggered when the user kills an application and all of its processes. The data will contain the name of the package, and it will also include the extra EXTRA_UID.
ACTION_PACKAGE_REMOVED	1+	A protected broadcast intent that can only be sent by the system and is triggered when an application has been removed from the device. As the application has been removed, it will not receive the intent. In addition to the data attribute containing the name of the application, the following extras will also be included: EXTRA_UID, EXTRA_DATA_REMOVED, and EXTRA_REPLACING.
ACTION_POWER_CONNECTED	4+	A protected broadcast intent that can only be sent by the system and indicates that the device has been connected to a power source.
ACTION_POWER_DISCONNECTED	4+	A protected broadcast intent that can only be sent by the system and indicates that the device has been disconnected from a power source.
ACTION_REBOOT	1+	A protected broadcast intent that can only be sent by the system and instructs the device to reboot.
ACTION_RUN	1+	A high-level action to run the defined data.

(continued)

35

Table 4-1. (*continued*)

Name	API Level	Description
ACTION_SCREEN_OFF	1+	A protected broadcast intent that can only be sent by the system and is sent when the device screen goes to sleep or becomes inactive.
ACTION_SHUTDOWN	4+	A protected broadcast intent that can only be sent by the system and is triggered during the device shutdown process.
ACTION_SEND	1+	A high-level action to send data to a recipient. It is common for this action to be paired a chooser.
ACTION_SET_WALLPAPER	1+	Used for displaying the settings for choosing a wallpaper.
ACTION_TIMEZONE_CHANGED	1+	A protected broadcast intent that can only be sent by the system and indicates that the system time zone has changed. The extra EXTRA_TIMEZONE is included.
ACTION_VOICE_COMMAND	1+	An intent action used to initiate a voice command.
ACTION_WEB_SEARCH	1+	An intent action used to initiate a web search.

Categories

Settable using an initialized `Intent` object's `addCategory` method. The `getCategories` method can also be used for retrieving a received intent's categories. Categories provide additional context about the action to be performed by the intent. Only activities that can facilitate all specified categories can be chosen to receive the intent.

An example of this can be seen here:

```
Intent intent = new Intent();
intent.addCategory(Intent.APP_CALCULATOR);
```

At the time of writing, the Android documentation[2] lists upward of 39 standard intent category attributes. Table 4-2 lists a subset of the most common of these intent categories.

Table 4-2. *Intent Categories*

Name	API Level	Description
CATEGORY_ ALTERNATIVE	1+	Used to identify an alternate action to the standard activity or the data the user is currently viewing.
CATEGORY_APP_ BROWSER	15+	Used to open an activity that should be able to browse the Internet. It can be used alongside `ACTION_MAIN` to open the preferred browser application.

(continued)

---

[2]"Intent | Android Open Source Project." 30 Nov. 2020, `https://developer. android.com/reference/android/content/Intent#flags`. Accessed 26 Dec. 2020.

Table 4-2. (*continued*)

Name	API Level	Description
CATEGORY_APP_ CALCULATOR	15+	Used to open an activity that should be able to perform standard arithmetic operations. It can be used alongside ACTION_MAIN to open the calculator application.
CATEGORY_APP_ CALENDAR	15+	Used to open an activity that should be able to perform standard calendar operations. It can be used alongside ACTION_MAIN to open the calendar application.
CATEGORY_APP_ CONTACTS	15+	Used to open an activity that should be able to view and manipulate address book entries. It can be used alongside ACTION_MAIN to open the contacts application.
CATEGORY_APP_ EMAIL	15+	Used to open an activity that should be able to send and receive email. It can be used alongside ACTION_MAIN to open the email application.
CATEGORY_APP_ FILES	15+	Used to open an activity that should be able to manage files stored on the device. It can be used alongside ACTION_MAIN to open the files application.
CATEGORY_APP_ GALLERY	15+	Used to open an activity that should be able to view and manipulate image and video files stored on the device. It can be used alongside ACTION_ MAIN to open the gallery application.
CATEGORY_APP_ MAPS	15+	Used to open an activity that should be able to show the user's current location. It can be used alongside ACTION_MAIN to open the maps application.

(*continued*)

Table 4-2. (*continued*)

Name	API Level	Description
CATEGORY_APP_MARKET	11+	Used to open an activity that should allow the user to browse and install new applications.
CATEGORY_APP_MESSAGING	15+	Used to open an activity that should be able to send and receive text messages. It can be used alongside ACTION_MAIN to open the messaging application.
CATEGORY_APP_MUSIC	15+	Used to open an activity that should be able to play music on the device. It can be used alongside ACTION_MAIN to open the music application.
CATEGORY_BROWSABLE	1+	Indicates activities that can be called and started directly from a browser (e.g., by a user selecting a link to the Google Play Store website and being taken to the Google Play Store application instead).
CATEGORY_CAR_MODE	8+	Indicates that the activity has been optimized to work in car environments.
CATEGORY_DEFAULT	1+	Used to identify activities that could be used as the default action.
CATEGORY_HOME	1+	The activity that launches when the device is started and whenever the user returns to the starting activity.
CATEGORY_LAUNCHER	1+	Used to identify an activity that can be used as the initial activity on a device (i.e., the home screen).
CATEGORY_MONKEY	1+	Indicates an activity that can be tested by monkey (an Android UI fuzzer) or other automated tools.

Extras

Settable using an initialized `Intent` object's `putExtra` method. The `getExtras` method can also be used for retrieving a received intent's extras. An extra is a bundle (a set of key-value pairs with varying types) which the receiver can use (e.g., when sharing a note with your social media app, the note text will be sent across as a field in a bundle). This bundle can include proprietary keys or ones set in the Android system such as `EXTRA_ALARM_COUNT`.

An example of this can be seen here:

```
Intent intent = new Intent();
intent.putExtra(Intent.EXTRA_TEXT, "This is an example text
extra");
```

At the time of writing, the Android documentation[3] lists upward of 80 standard intent extra attributes. Table 4-3 lists a subset of the most common of these intent extras.

---

[3]"Intent | Android Open Source Project." 30 Nov. 2020, `https://developer. android.com/reference/android/content/Intent#flags`. Accessed 26 Dec. 2020.

Table 4-3. *Intent Extras*

Name	API Level	Description
EXTRA_CHANGED_ COMPONENT_NAME_ LIST	7+	Part of the intent action ACTION_ PACKAGE_CHANGED and contains a string array of all of the components that have changed.
EXTRA_DONT_KILL_ APP	1+	Part of the ACTION_PACKAGE_REMOVED and ACTION_PACKAGE_CHANGED actions and overrides the default behavior of restarting the targeted application.
EXTRA_DATA_ REMOVED	3+	Part of the ACTION_PACKAGE_REMOVED action and is used to indicate that the remove should be a full uninstall, removing both data and code instead of a partial uninstall which leaves the data (the latter is performed as part of an update).
EXTRA_HTML_TEXT	16+	Can be used as part of the ACTION_SEND action alongside the EXTRA_TEXT extra and indicates that the extra text is HTML-formatted text.
EXTRA_MIME_TYPES	19+	Used to set acceptable MIME types (e.g., audio/mpeg or audio/*).
EXTRA_NOT_ UNKNOWN_SOURCE	14+	Part of the ACTION_INSTALL_PACKAGE action and indicates that the application to be installed is being installed from the application sending the intent and not an unknown source.

(continued)

Table 4-3. (*continued*)

Name	API Level	Description
EXTRA_PACKAGE_ NAME	24+	Contains an application name.
EXTRA_PHONE_ NUMBER	1+	Part of the ACTION_NEW_OUTGOING_CALL and ACTION_CALL actions and contains the phone number for the call.
EXTRA_QUIET_MODE	24+	Indicates whether quiet mode (where all applications in the profile are killed) has been switched on or off.
EXTRA_REFERRER	17+	Used when an intent is launching an activity to identify who initiated the launch. Value is provided as a URI.
EXTRA_REPLACING	3+	Used as part of the ACTION_PACKAGE_ REMOVED action to indicate that the package has been replaced.
EXTRA_REFERRER_ NAME	22+	Alternative to the EXTRA_REFERRER extra; however, the value is provided as a string instead of a URI.
EXTRA_SHUTDOWN_ USERSPACE_ONLY	19+	Used as part of the ACTION_SHUTDOWN action to identify that a partial shutdown should be performed. This partial shutdown solely restarts user space instead of performing a full OS restart.
EXTRA_SUBJECT	1+	A high level extra containing a subject for the data being sent.

(*continued*)

Table 4-3. (*continued*)

Name	API Level	Description
EXTRA_TEXT	1+	Part of the ACTION_SEND action. A high level extra containing data to be received in the form of a CharSequence (or String as String implements the CharSequence interface).
EXTRA_TIME	30+	A high-level extra where its value contains a time in milliseconds since the Epoch (e.g., 1608553466).
EXTRA_TIMEZONE	30+	Part of the ACTION_TIMEZONE_CHANGED action indicating the device's time zone.
EXTRA_TITLE	1+	Part of the ACTION_CHOOSER to provide a title to the user (CharSequence, String, etc.).
EXTRA_UID	1+	Part of the ACTION_UID_REMOVED, ACTION_PACKAGE_REMOVED, and ACTION_PACKAGE_CHANGED use to identify the application being operated on.

Flags

Settable using an initialized Intent object's setFlag method. Flags represent the behavior of the component being launched (e.g., not including the launched activity in the task stack). The getFlags method can also be used for retrieving a received intent's flags.

An example of this can be seen here:

```
Intent intent = new Intent();
intent.setFlags(Intent.FLAG_ACTIVITY_NEW_TASK);
```

At the time of writing, the Android documentation[4] lists upward of 35 intent flags. Table 4-4 shows a subset of the most common of these intent flags.

Table 4-4. *Intent Flags*

Name	API Level	Description
EXCLUDE_STOPPED_ PACKAGES	12+	The default behavior of the Android system is to consider all applications on a device when choosing an applicable component to launch. If this flag is set stopped, packages will not be included.
FLAG_ACTIVITY_NO_ HISTORY	1+	If set, the new activity does not remain in the history stack after the activity is left by the user (e.g., the user traversing to another application).
FLAG_ACTIVITY_ PREVIOUS_IS_TOP	1+	When using this flag, the previous activity remains at the top of the task stack for deciding where new intents are sent to.

(continued)

---

[4]"Intent | Android Open Source Project." 30 Nov. 2020, `https://developer.android.com/reference/android/content/Intent#flags`. Accessed 26 Dec. 2020.

Table 4-4. (*continued*)

Name	API Level	Description
FLAG_ACTIVITY_ SINGLE_TOP	1+	When set, if the activity receiving the intent is already at the top of the task stack, then no action occurs.
FLAG_ACTIVITY_ NEW_TASK	11+	Using this flag creates a new group of activities that a user can traverse to with a separate task stack.
FLAG_ACTIVITY_NO_ ANIMATION	5+	When set no transition animation will be applied to the starting of the specific activity.
FLAG_ACTIVITY_CLEAR_ TOP	1+	If set and the activity being started is already in the current task stack, then all other activities in the stack are removed and replaced by the new activity.
FLAG_ACTIVITY_ EXCLUDE_FROM_RECENTS	1+	If set the started activity is not included in the system list of recently started applications.

Task Stack

Also known as the back stack, this is a last-in-first-out stack that stores a logical list of activities for user traversal. When an application is launched and no tasks for it currently exist, the activity with the MAIN action in the application's manifest is launched. When this activity comes to the foreground, it creates a new root on the task stack (as seen in Figures 4-1 and 4-2). Each subsequent activity that is started is placed onto the task stack, and when the user selects the back button, these activities are popped off the stack. Each application can have one or multiple task stacks depending on the specific flags that were set when starting the activity.

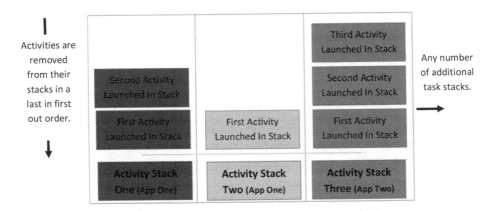

Figure 4-1. *Example of Android task stack*

When a task is not in the foreground (e.g., the home screen button has been pressed or the user traverses to another application/task stack), the activity at the top of the stack enters the onPause() state and moves to the background. Multiple tasks can exist simultaneously in the background; however, the system may destroy these tasks if it needs to preserve memory.

It is also important to note that applications can run in the background without being present in the task stack, via the use of services and other long-running utilities; this is described further in Chapter 9.

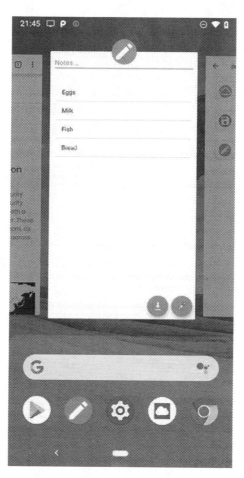

Figure 4-2. *Multiple task stacks viewed in the UI*

Intent Filters

All components should have an android:exported tag. This is false
by default, and if it is false, then the component can only receive
messages from inside of its application. By adding any intent filters, this
is automatically true and means that external applications can interact
with the component. These intent filters are also used to advertise the
component when the system receives an implicit intent, and it decides

which applications can receive the intent. There are three main types of intent filters, these being Action, Data, and Category (as described previously).

The following is an example of a typical entry point to an application with the MAIN action and LAUNCHER category set. The main action defines that this component should be started as the entry point to the application and that it does not receive any data. The launcher category defines that the activity should be displayed in the top-level launcher.

An example intent filter for an entry point activity to an application:

```
<intent-filter>
    <action android:name="android.intent.action.MAIN" />
    <category android:name="android.intent.category.LAUNCHER" />
</intent-filter>
```

Starting an internal activity with data:

```
public void sendIntentToActivityInApp(){
    Intent intent= new Intent(this, IntentReceiver.class);
    // Update class to be internal class (to the application)
        to receive the intent
    Bundle bundle= new Bundle();
    bundle.putString("key", "value");
    intent.putExtras(bundle);
    startActivity(intent);
}
```

Receiving an intent bundle in an activity:

```
protected void onCreate(@Nullable Bundle savedInstanceState) {
    super.onCreate(savedInstanceState);

    if (getIntent().hasExtra("key")) {
      String value = getIntent().getExtras().getString("key");
      Log.v(this.getClass().getSimpleName(), value);
    }
}
```

Starting an external application:

```
public void startActivityViaIntent(){
    Intent launchIntent = getPackageManager().
    getLaunchIntentForPackage("com.android.chrome");
    startActivity(launchIntent);
}
```

Starting a specific activity of an external application:

```
public void sendIntentToAnotherActivity(){
    Intent intent = new Intent();
    intent.setClassName("com.android.chrome", "com.google.
    android.apps.chrome.Main");
    intent.setFlags(Intent.FLAG_ACTIVITY_NEW_TASK) ;

    startActivity(intent);
}
```

Sending a file to another activity. As of API level 24, sending files to other applications requires a file provider so that a custom URI can be shared:

```
public void sendFileToAnoutherApplication(){
    File file =new File(getApplicationContext().
    getFilesDir(),"/text/test.txt");
    writeFileInInternalStorage(file, "Hello World");

    Intent intent = new Intent(Intent.ACTION_SEND);

    Uri contentUri = getUriForFile(getApplicationContext(),
    "com.example.intents.fileprovider", file);
    intent.setType("text/plain");

    intent.putExtra(Intent.EXTRA_STREAM,contentUri);

    startActivity(Intent.createChooser(intent , "File path"));
 }
```

Implicit phone number intent:

```
public void phoneNumberIntent(){
    Uri number = Uri.parse("tel:5551234");
    Intent callIntent = new Intent(Intent.ACTION_DIAL, number);
    startActivity(callIntent);
}
```

Implicit URL intent:

```
public void webIntent(){
    Uri webpage = Uri.parse("https://www.android.com");
    Intent webIntent = new Intent(Intent.ACTION_VIEW, webpage);
    startActivity(webIntent);
}
```

CHAPTER 5

Application Names, Android Package Name, and ID

Android uses multiple naming conventions to uniquely identify an Android application; these have been summarized in the following and broken down into more detail in this chapter:

- **Java Package Name** - Set in the code base and depicts the folder structure of the project and structure of an application and helps to modularize application components. This is used for differentiating classes in multiple packages with the same name as well as being used by techniques such as reflection. It uses reverse Internet domain convention, such as `com.mywebsite.blog`.

- **Package ID** - Set in the manifest file via the package attribute. This is used by the Google Play Store and Android system. This has to match the Java Package Name. It uses reverse Internet domain convention, such as `com.mywebsite.blog`.

© James Stevenson 2021
J. Stevenson, *Android Software Internals Quick Reference*,
https://doi.org/10.1007/978-1-4842-6914-5_5

- **Application ID** - Set in the Gradle build file and replaces Package ID in the manifest file post-build. It doesn't have to match Package ID or Java Package Name. It uses reverse Internet domain convention, such as `com.mywebsite.blog`.

- **Application Name** - A name not following the reverse Internet domain convention (and so can be a string such as *myappname*) and is shown to the end user.

None of these values can be changed programmatically. This is because they are either already compiled (in the case of the Java Package Name) or located in the manifest or res folder (which are read-only) in the case of Package ID, Application ID, and Application Name.

Java Package Name

The Java Package Name[1] is a unique series of lowercase (to avoid clashes with interface or class names) strings written in reverse Internet domain convention. It is set in each class file (as seen in the following) and depicts the folder structure of the project and structure of an application and helps to modularize application components. In turn the Java Package Name is also used for how Java techniques such as reflection interact with the application. An example of a Java Package Name for a banking application belonging to the website `jamesstevenson.me` could be `me.jamesstevenson.banking`.

---

[1]"Naming a Package (The Java™ Tutorials > Learning the Java ....)" `https://docs.oracle.com/javase/tutorial/java/package/namingpkgs.html`. Accessed 11 May. 2020.

An example activity:

```
package me.jamesstevenson.banking;

import androidx.appcompat.app.AppCompatActivity;
import android.os.Bundle;

public class MainActivity extends AppCompatActivity {

    @Override
    protected void onCreate(Bundle savedInstanceState) {
        super.onCreate(savedInstanceState);
        setContentView(R.layout.activity_main);
    }
}
```

Because of the following identifiers, in Android there are very few reasons (outside of reflection) to share an application's package name externally to the code base.

Package ID

An application's Package ID is set in the AndroidManifest.xml package attribute and has to match the Java Package Name. If using Gradle build tools, the Package ID is replaced by the Application ID after the build has occurred. This is used as part of the build process in generating the namespace for the R.java class (used for resource handling) as well as in resolving relative class names (such as .MainActivity to com.example.example_app.MainActivity). After the build this is used by the Google Play Store and the Android system as described in the Android ID section.

Example of Package ID in Android manifest:

```
<manifest xmlns:android="http://schemas.android.com/apk/res/
android"
    package="com.example.android_namings">
```

As stated the Package ID can be edited directly in the *AndroidManifest.xml* file by changing the package element; however, if using Gradle to build and you want your package ID to be maintained post-build, make sure to remove the Application ID element in your `build.gradle` file, as mentioned in the following, as otherwise it will be replaced.

Retrieving Package ID

While none of these identifiers can be changed programmatically, they can be accessed. This retrieves the value of the Package ID as it was during build.

Example of retrieving the Package ID:

```
Log.v("PackageID BuildConfig", BuildConfig.APPLICATION_ID);
Log.v("PackageID context", getApplicationContext().
getPackageName());
```

Application ID

In addition to the Package ID, when using Gradle and the Android Build Tools, you can also set an Application ID.

There are three rules that cover the creation of an Application ID name:

- It must have at least two segments (one or more dots).

- Each segment must start with a letter.

- All characters must be alphanumeric or an underscore [a-zA-Z0-9_].

The Application ID is set in the Gradle `build.gradle` file via the `applicationId` attribute. The Application ID can differ to your Package ID, and in turn to your Java Package Name.

Figure 5-1. *Google Play Store listing*

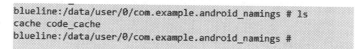

Figure 5-2. *Application's internal storage file path*

This Application ID replaces an application's Package ID post build, in turn allowing the Package ID to be used in the build process and then replacing it so that the Application ID is used by the Google Play Store (as seen in Figure 5-1) and Android system (as seen in Figure 5-2). As stated previously this is so that the internal Java Package Name is not shared outside of the program's code base. With this in mind in the example where the Java Package Name is com.example.internalname, however, the Application Name needs to be visible as com.example.appname in the Google Play Store; the Package ID in the AndroidManifest.xml file would need to be set to com.example.internalname and the applicationId attribute in the build.gradle file set to com.example.appname.

In the circumstance where Gradle isn't being used, the Java Package Name would need to be refactored to match com.example.appname, and the Package ID attribute in AndroidManifest.xml would need to be set to com.example.appname also.

Setting Application ID in Gradle build file:

```
defaultConfig {
    applicationId "com.example.appname"
    minSdkVersion 16
    targetSdkVersion 29
    versionCode 1
    versionName "1.0"

    testInstrumentationRunner "androidx.test.runner.
AndroidJUnitRunner"
}
```

Suffix and Flavor

In addition to the fact that the Application ID and Package ID can be different, you can also create different suffixes for your Android projects - named product flavors. The common use for this is in having a different Application ID for different versions (such as paid and trial) of an application. The suffix can be modified in the applications build.gradle file.

Modifying the suffix and flavor in the Gradle build file:

```
android {
    defaultConfig {
        applicationId "com.example.appname"
    }
    productFlavors {
        free {
            applicationIdSuffix ".trial"
        }
        pro {
            applicationIdSuffix ".paid"
        }
    }
}
```

Application Name

The Application Name in Android is what is visible to the end user
(as can be seen in Figures 5-3 Figure 5-4); this is what is shown on the
application's setting's page and what is shown by default underneath the
application icon (however, the application icon and text can be switched
out programmatically in some cases[2]).

---

[2]"How to programmatically change your Android app icon and ...." 29 Apr. 2019,
https://blog.jakelee.co.uk/programmatically-changing-app-icon/.
Accessed 11 May. 2020.

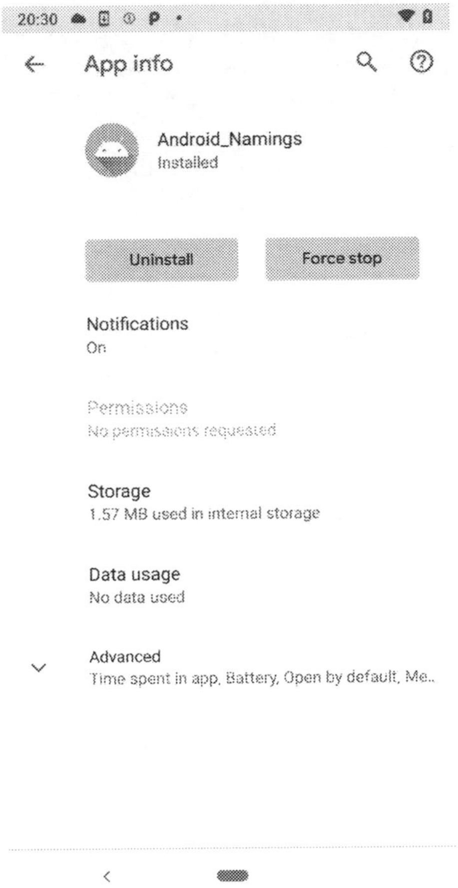

Figure 5-3. *Application setting's page*

Figure 5-4. *Application icon and title*

Setting the Application Name can be done by editing the `label` attribute in the `AndroidManifest.xml` file, as seen in the following. The best practice is for this to link to a `String` in the string resource; however, this does not have to be the case.

Setting the Application Name in the Android manifest file:

```
android:label="My Application Name"
```

Retrieving Application Name

The Application Name can be retrieved programmatically:

```
public static String getApplicationName(Context context) {
    ApplicationInfo applicationInfo = context.
    getApplicationInfo();
    int stringId = applicationInfo.labelRes;
    return stringId == 0 ? applicationInfo.nonLocalizedLabel.
    toString() : context.getString(stringId);
}
```

CHAPTER 6

Storage

Partitions

Android (as of Android 2.2) uses the ext4 file system, which at its core follows the Linux file system structure - using a single root denoted by /.

In the Android root, there are several key partitions;[1, 2] these partitions can be listed by using the following command in the Android shell:

```
cat /proc/mounts
```

---

[1]"Partitions and Images | Android Open Source Project." 6 Jan. 2020, https://source.android.com/devices/bootloader/partitions-images. Accessed 11 May. 2020.

[2]"Android File System." http://www.uobabylon.edu.iq/eprints/publication_4_13681_1356.pdf. Accessed 11 May. 2020.

© James Stevenson 2021
J. Stevenson, *Android Software Internals Quick Reference*,
https://doi.org/10.1007/978-1-4842-6914-5_6

Depending on the device version, original design manufacturer,[3] and original equipment manufacturer, the specific folders both mounted and present at the root of the filesystem may vary. That being the case, some of the most common folders that may be present are listed here:

- **/boot** - The boot partition includes both the RAM disk and a kernel image. Both of these are bundled via `mkbootimg`[4] which is a utility used for packing boot images. The device will not boot without this partition.

- **/system** - This partition covers the Android framework. This includes the Android GUI and system applications - available at `/system/app` and `/system/priv-app`. Wiping this partition removes Android from the device while remaining bootable.

- **/vendor** - This partition includes binaries and resources that aren't included in the stock AOSP[5] (primarily focusing on kernel modules for board-specific components, board-specific daemons, or additional features for the hardware abstraction layers (HALs)). This partition is primarily for the original design manufacturer (such as Qualcomm, Exynos, and Huawei) to add custom binaries and GUIs.

---

[3]"Building ODM Partitions | Android Open Source Project." 6 Jan. 2020, `https://source.android.com/devices/bootloader/odm-partitions`. Accessed 11 May. 2020.

[4]"Android: Boot image - Compulab Mediawiki." 21 Oct. 2015, `https://mediawiki.compulab.com/index.php/Android:_Boot_image`. Accessed 11 May. 2020.

[5]"Android Open Source Project." `https://source.android.com/`. Accessed 11 May. 2020.

As of Android 8, it was enforced[6] that when these components are added to a device by an ODM (original design manufacturers) or OEM (original equipment manufacturer), they should be added to the /vendor partition over the /system partition, which was the location commonly used before this was enforced.

- **/odm** - An extension of the /vendor partition, designed for the original design manufacturer.[7] This partition allows for multiple devices to be made with the same /vendor partition and for the /odm partition to provide minor changes between them. Similar to the /system partition in this partition, there are also locations for applications (/odm/app/), native libraries (/odm/lib[64]), and more. Full support for this partition was added in Android 10.

- **/oem** - Original equipment manufacturers[8] (such as Samsung, OnePlus, and Huawei) may decide to make changes to the AOSP image - for example, adding their own applications, UIs, or features. An extension to this is the /product partition which was added in Android 9, which unlike the OEM partition is updatable.

- **/recovery** - This partition stores the recovery image.

---

[6]"Building Product Partitions | Android Open Source Project." 6 Jan. 2020, https://source.android.com/devices/bootloader/product-partitions. Accessed 11 May. 2020.

[7]"Building ODM Partitions | Android Open Source Project." 6 Jan. 2020, https://source.android.com/devices/bootloader/odm-partitions. Accessed 11 May. 2020.

[8]"Building Product Partitions | Android Open Source Project." 6 Jan. 2020, https://source.android.com/devices/bootloader/product-partitions. Accessed 11 May. 2020.

- **/data** - Called the user-data partition, this partition includes the internal storage for applications (e.g., /data/user/0/com.android.chrome) as well as containing the /data/local/tmp directory and other types of user data. As of Android 5, Android has supported having multiple users on the same device; this means that different users' internal storage will be available at different locations (e.g., /data/user/0/ com.android.chrome and /data/user/1/com.android. chrome). As part of a factory reset, this partition is wiped.

- **/cache** - This partition is where Android stores frequently used components as well as where some data is stored as part of over the air updates.

- **/misc** - Miscellaneous system settings, normally in the form of on/off switches.

- **/metadata** - The metadata partition is used when the device is encrypted.

- **/radio** - This partition is only used when the device includes a radio component.

- **/tos** - This partition contains the binary image of the Trusty OS.

- **/sdcard** - Prior to Android 4, this directory was the location where the storage for a connected SD card could be found. As of Android 4, this changed to what is referred to as the "internal SD card" (where the SD card mount moved to /sdcard_ext or /sdcard/external_sd). This is also referred to as the device's external storage (irrespective of if it refers to an actual SD card or not) and is discussed more below.

External and Internal Storage

Internal Storage

Each application has its own internal storage space for storing arbitrary data. This space does not require any permissions to write to and is sandboxed to each application - meaning that one application cannot read the internal storage of another application.

An application's internal storage is located at the following path (replacing 0 with the Android user ID):

```
/data/user/0/<Package ID>/
```

The structure of an application's internal storage is by default broken down into a handful of subdirectories; however, arbitrary folders can be added to this space. While this storage has no restrictions on it, it is recommended to store specific file types in specific directories; however, it is not enforced.

- **/files** - The files directory is used for arbitrary files. These can be text files, images, serialized files like JSON, or any other file type. To retrieve a file path to this directory, use `getApplicationContext(). getFilesDir()`.

- **/databases** - The database directory is used for storing databases. Android has a lot of inbuilt support for creating and managing SQLite databases; however, other database types such as Realm databases[9] can be stored here. When creating these types of databases, by default this is the directory they're saved to.

---

[9]"Realm: Create reactive mobile apps in a fraction of the time." `https://realm.io/`. Accessed 11 May. 2020.

- **/shared_prefs** - Shared preferences are Android's take
  on easily accessible key-value pairs. These are saved in
  an XML format. When creating shared preferences, this
  is the directory that they're saved to.

- **/cache** - The cache directory[10] is designed for saving
  temporary files, as the Android system will delete files
  in this folder when space is needed elsewhere on the
  device. The cache directory can be accessed using
  the application context: `getApplicationContext().`
  `getCacheDir()`.

- **/lib** - Used for storing shared library files.

- **/code_cache** - Similar to the cache directory, and
  added in API level 21, this directory is designed for
  storing cached code. Like the cache directory, it is also
  cleared by the Android system if space is required.
  The path to this directory can be retrieved with the
  application context: `getApplicationContext().`
  `getCodeCacheDir()`.

- **/no_backup** - Similar to the /files directory, however,
  files stored in this directory will be excluded from
  automatic backup facilities.[11]

The path to an application's internal storage can be retrieved by using
the application context. It's important to bear in mind that these file paths
could change over time and from OS version to OS version, and so storing
a hardcoded path is not recommended.

---

[10]"Context | Android Developers." `https://developer.android.com/reference/`
`android/content/Context`. Accessed 11 May. 2020.

[11]"Android - platform/frameworks/base - Android GoogleSource." `https://`
`android.googlesource.com/platform/frameworks/base/+/a7835b6%5E!/`.
Accessed 11 May. 2020.

From API level 24 and later, the following can be used to retrieve the file path to the root of an application's internal storage:

```
getApplicationContext().getDataDir();
```

Before API level 24, the following can be used:

```
getApplicationContext().getFilesDir().getParent();
```

External Storage

As noted earlier, prior to Android 4, the `/sdcard` directory was the location where the storage for a connected SD card could be found. As of Android 4, this changed to what is referred to as the "internal SD card" or more commonly "external storage,"[12] which is a shared space across applications. As of Android 10, this "shared space" has changed to a term referred to as scoped storage;[13] this means that even if an application has access to external storage (requiring either the `READ_EXTERNAL_STORAGE` or `WRITE_EXTERNAL_STORAGE` permission), it will now only have read only access as well as access to an application-specific directory as well as specific types of media that the app has created (unless it has access to the `MANAGE_EXTERNAL_STORAGE` permission). In addition to this, on devices with multiple users, they are each provided with their own isolated scoped storage.

With this in mind if targeting and compiling for API level 28 or below, then you can use the `Environment` class to retrieve the path to the device's external storage. However if running on API level 29 and above, this is deprecated, and the file path returned will not be accessible, so the application *Context* should be used instead (for scoped storage).

---

[12]"Security tips | Android Developers." 3 Jun. 2019, `https://developer.android.com/training/articles/security-tips`. Accessed 11 May. 2020.

[13]"Data and file storage overview | Android Developers." 3 Jun. 2019, `https://developer.android.com/training/data-storage`. Accessed 11 May. 2020.

Get global external storage (API levels 1–28):

```
Environment.getExternalStorageDirectory();
```

Get application scoped (sandboxed) external storage (API level 29+):

```
getApplicationContext().getExternalFilesDir(null);
```

Unlike internal storage, if an application wants to write or read a file to the global external storage, it requires the `WRITE_EXTERNAL_STORAGE` or `READ_EXTERNAL_STORAGE` permission. Writing to external storage is a runtime (dangerous) permission, while reading is only a normal/manifest permission. No permissions are required for scoped storage.

The following is an example of setting manifest permissions:

```
<uses-permission android:name="android.permission.WRITE_
EXTERNAL_STORAGE" />
<uses-permission android:name="android.permission.READ_
EXTERNAL_STORAGE" />
```

As writing to the external storage is a dangerous permission, it requires the user to accept a runtime permission before the application is giving access. This will display a notification to the user as can be seen in Figure 6-1.

An external storage write runtime request can be run with the following code.

```
if (Build.VERSION.SDK_INT >= 23) {
    if (!isStoragePermissionGranted()){
        ActivityCompat.requestPermissions(this, new String[]
        {Manifest.permission.WRITE_EXTERNAL_STORAGE}, 1234567);
    }
}
```

An example method that checks if the WRITE_EXTERNAL_STORAGE runtime permission is already set:

```
public  boolean isStoragePermissionGranted() {
    if (Build.VERSION.SDK_INT >= Build.VERSION_CODES.M) {
        if (checkSelfPermission(android.Manifest.permission.
        WRITE_EXTERNAL_STORAGE)
                == PackageManager.PERMISSION_GRANTED) {
            Log.v(TAG,"Permission is granted");
            return true;
        } else {

            Log.v(TAG,"Permission is revoked");
            ActivityCompat.requestPermissions(this, new
            String[]{Manifest.permission.WRITE_EXTERNAL_
            STORAGE}, 1);
            return false;
        }
    }
    else { //permission is automatically granted on sdk<23 upon
            installation
        Log.v(TAG,"Permission is granted");
        return true;
    }
}
```

The activity callback that is executed when the permission changes:

```
@Override
public void onRequestPermissionsResult(int requestCode,
String[] permissions, int[] grantResults) {
    super.onRequestPermissionsResult(requestCode, permissions,
    grantResults);
```

```
if(grantResults.length > 0 && grantResults[0] ==
PackageManager.PERMISSION_GRANTED){
    Log.v(TAG,"Permission: "+permissions[0]+ " was
    "+grantResults[0]);
    //write file to external storage
}
}
```

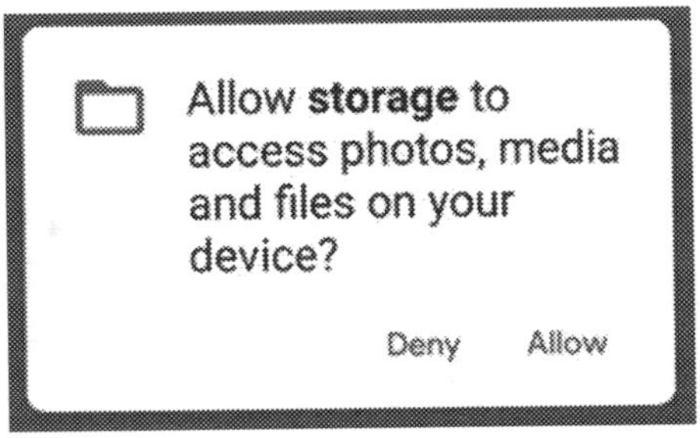

Figure 6-1. *Runtime permission dialogue box*

Text Files

Files can be written to anywhere in an application's internal or external storage (bearing in mind scoped storage as of Android 10). The location of these directories can be retrieved with the aforementioned method calls.

To make a File object that operates on a specific file, use the following code where filename is a String object representing the path to the file:

```
String filename = "myFile.txt";
File file = new File(getApplicationContext().getFilesDir(),
filename);
```

Writing a file:

```
public void writeFileInInternalStorage(File fileToWrite,
String fileBody){

    // If file doesn't exist attempt to make full
       directory path
    if(!fileToWrite.exists()){
        fileToWrite.getParentFile().mkdir();
    }

    // Write to file
    try{
        FileWriter writer = new FileWriter(fileToWrite);
        writer.append(fileBody);
        writer.flush();
        writer.close();

    }catch (Exception e){
        e.printStackTrace();

    }
}
```

Reading a file:

```
private String readFromFile(File file) {

    String ret = "";

    try {
        FileInputStream inputStream = new
        FileInputStream(file);
```

```
            if ( inputStream != null ) {
                InputStreamReader inputStreamReader = new Input
                StreamReader(inputStream);
                BufferedReader bufferedReader = new Buffered
                Reader(inputStreamReader);
                String receiveString = "";
                StringBuilder stringBuilder = new
                StringBuilder();

                while ( (receiveString = bufferedReader.
                readLine()) != null ) {
                    stringBuilder.append("\n").append
                    (receiveString);
                }

                inputStream.close();
                ret = stringBuilder.toString();
            }
        }
        catch (FileNotFoundException e) {
            Log.e("TAG", "File not found: " + e.toString());
        } catch (IOException e) {
            Log.e("TAG", "Can not read file: " + e.toString());
        }

        return ret;
    }
```

Deleting a file:

```
private void deleteStorageFile(File file){
    file.delete();
}
```

Databases

The following details how to create a simple SQLite database in Android. In Android, databases are created, by default, in the /databases directory of internal storage.

Define a schema and contract:

```
public final class databaseTemplate {

    // Inner class that represents the table values
    public static class databaseData implements BaseColumns {
        public static final String TABLE_NAME = "TABLE_NAME";
        public static final String COLUMN_ONE = "FIRST_COLUMN_
        NAME";
        public static final String COLUMN_TWO = "SECOND_COLUMN_
        NAME";
    }
}
```

Creating a database helper:

```
public class databaseHelper extends SQLiteOpenHelper {

    public databaseHelper(Context context) {
        super(context, NAME, null, VERSION);
    }

    private static final String SQL_CREATE_INSTRUCTION =
        "CREATE TABLE " + databaseTemplate.databaseData.TABLE_
        NAME + " (" + databaseTemplate.databaseData._ID +
        " INTEGER PRIMARY KEY," +
            databaseTemplate.databaseData.COLUMN_ONE + " TEXT," +
            databaseTemplate.databaseData.COLUMN_TWO + " TEXT)";
```

```
private static final String SQL_DELETE_INSTRUCTION =
    "DROP TABLE IF EXISTS " + databaseTemplate.
    databaseData.TABLE_NAME;

public static final int VERSION = 1; //increment if schema
changed

public static final String NAME = "database.db";
// database name

// Standard Database functions

public void onCreate(SQLiteDatabase database) {
    database.execSQL(SQL_CREATE_INSTRUCTION);
}

public void onUpgrade(SQLiteDatabase database, int
previousVersion, int currentVersion) {
    database.execSQL(SQL_DELETE_INSTRUCTION);
    onCreate(database);
}
}
```

Adding a row to a database:

```
private void addDataToDatabase(Context context, String
columnOneData, String columnTwoData){

    databaseHelper databaseHelper = new
    databaseHelper(context);

    SQLiteDatabase database = databaseHelper.
    getWritableDatabase();
```

```
ContentValues contentValues = new ContentValues();
contentValues.put(databaseTemplate.databaseData.COLUMN_ONE,
columnOneData);
contentValues.put(databaseTemplate.databaseData.COLUMN_TWO,
columnTwoData);

database.insert(databaseTemplate.databaseData.TABLE_NAME,
null, contentValues);
}
```

Reading a database:

```
private List readFromDatabase(Context context){

    final String TABLE_NAME = databaseTemplate.databaseData.
    TABLE_NAME;

    String selectQuery = "SELECT * FROM " + TABLE_NAME;
    databaseHelper databaseHelper = new
    databaseHelper(context);
    SQLiteDatabase database = databaseHelper.
    getWritableDatabase();
    Cursor cursor = database.rawQuery(selectQuery, null);
    ArrayList data = new ArrayList();

    if (cursor.moveToFirst()) {
        do {
            int idIndex = cursor.getColumnIndexOrThrow(database
            Template.databaseData._ID);
            int columnOneIndex = cursor.getColumnIndexOrThrow
            (databaseTemplate.databaseData.COLUMN_ONE);
            int columnTwoIndex = cursor.getColumnIndexOrThrow
            (databaseTemplate.databaseData.COLUMN_TWO);
```

```
            String idValue = String.valueOf(cursor.getString
            (idIndex));
            String columnOneValue = String.valueOf(cursor.
            getString(columnOneIndex));
            String columnTwoValue = String.valueOf(cursor.
            getString(columnTwoIndex));

            ArrayList rowData = new ArrayList();
            rowData.add(idValue);
            rowData.add(columnOneValue);
            rowData.add(columnTwoValue);

            data.add(rowData);
        } while (cursor.moveToNext());
    }
    cursor.close();

    return data;
}
```

Deleting a row from a database:

```
private void deleteRowFromDatabase(Context context,
int rowIdToRemove){

    databaseHelper databaseHelper = new databaseHelper
    (context);
    SQLiteDatabase database = databaseHelper.
    getReadableDatabase();

    String selection = databaseTemplate.databaseData._ID + "
    LIKE ?";

    String[] selectionValues = {String.valueOf(rowIdToRemove)};

    database.delete(databaseTemplate.databaseData.TABLE_NAME,
    selection, selectionValues);
}
```

Shared Preferences

Shared preferences[14] are written to the /shared_prefs directory in an application's internal storage. These take the form of XML key-value pairs where the shared preference name becomes the name of the XML file (appended with .xml).

As can be seen in the following, there are two entries in this shared preference, one of type long *called* last_cleanup *and the other of type* string *called* webapp_name:

```
<?xml version='1.0' encoding='utf-8' standalone='yes' ?>
<map>
    <long name="last_cleanup" value="1585307669741" />
    <string name="webapp_name"  value="webapp"/>
</map>
```

Shared preferences accept the primitive data types of

- String
- Int
- Boolean
- Long
- Float
- String set

---

[14]"Save key-value data | Android Developers." 3 Jun. 2019, https://developer.android.com/training/data-storage/shared-preferences. Accessed 11 May. 2020.

When creating a shared preference, you must provide the name of the shared preference; this is the name of the XML file. In addition to this, you will need to provide the key-value pair to be saved to the shared preference, and then either use `.apply()` (added in API level 8) for asynchronous or `.commit()` for synchronous (which returns a Boolean indicating success) saving. In addition to this, you must also provide the mode. The mode is an integer and represents one of the following:

- **MODE_PRIVATE** - The default mode where the file can only be accessed by the application that created it.

- **MODE_WORLD_READABLE** - Deprecated in API level 17 and throws a *SecurityException* starting with API level 24. This allowed all applications to have read access to the created file.

- **MODE_WORLD_WRITEABLE** - Deprecated in API level 17 and throws a *SecurityException* starting with API level 24. This allowed all other applications to have write access to the created file.

- **MODE_MULTI_PROCESS** - Deprecated in API level 23. Prior to API level 10, this was the default behavior. After this point the default behavior is for shared preferences to be loaded into memory and for reads and modifications to be performed on the in-memory shared preference. This means that if the original file was edited while the application was running, it would be written over by any changes the application made to the shared preference. When this mode is set, the shared preference will be checked for modification even if it is already loaded in memory.

Adding a key-value pair:

```
SharedPreferences sharedPref
        = getApplicationContext().getSharedPreferences
          ("MySharedPref",
        MODE_PRIVATE);
SharedPreferences.Editor editor = sharedPref.edit();
editor.putString("key", "value");
editor.apply();
```

When reading from a shared preference, you must provide a default value of the type being retrieved. This is returned if the provided key does not exist:

```
SharedPreferences sharedPref
        = getApplicationContext().getSharedPreferences("MyShare
          dPref",
        MODE_PRIVATE);
String value = sharedPref.getString("key", "default value");
```

Deleting a shared preference is similar to editing one; however, instead of using a .put method, the .remove() method is used instead:

```
SharedPreferences sharedPref = getSharedPreferences("MySharedPr
ef", MODE_PRIVATE);
SharedPreferences.Editor editor = sharedPref.edit();
editor.remove("key");
editor.apply();
```

File Providers

As of Android API level 24, you cannot directly share file URIs[15] with other applications. After this point you have to use a `FileProvider`[16] which are used to securely offer a file from your application[17] to another application.

In setting up a `FileProvider`, add a `provider` tag to the application's manifest file application tag that follows the format of the following bearing in mind to change the package name:

```
<provider
    android:name="androidx.core.content.FileProvider"
    android:authorities="com.example.storage.fileprovider"
    android:grantUriPermissions="true"
    android:exported="false">
    <meta-data
        android:name="android.support.FILE_PROVIDER_PATHS"
        android:resource="@xml/filepaths" />
</provider>
```

After this make an XML resource in your applications `res` directory, in a subfolder called `xml`, called `filepaths.xml.` Then define the path to share and the name that will be represented in the URI. The following example shares the entire root of the application's `myText` folder, where the URI would be `content://com.example.storage.fileprovider/myText`.

---

[15]"Sharing Content with Intents | CodePath Android Cliffnotes." `https://guides.codepath.com/android/Sharing-Content-with-Intents`. Accessed 11 May. 2020.

[16]"FileProvider | Android Developers." 27 Dec. 2019, `https://developer.android.com/reference/androidx/core/content/FileProvider`. Accessed 11 May. 2020.

[17]"Setting up file sharing | Android Developers." `https://developer.android.com/training/secure-file-sharing/setup-sharing`. Accessed 11 May. 2020.

The filepaths xml file in res should include:

```
<?xml version="1.0" encoding="utf-8"?>
<paths>
    <files-path path="/" name="myText" />
</paths>
```

After this a file (inside of the specified directory) can be sent via an intent as normal:

```
File file =new File(getApplicationContext().getFilesDir(),
"/myText/test.txt");
writeFileInInternalStorage(file, "Hello World");
// This function is referenced in the Text Files section.

Intent intent = new Intent(Intent.ACTION_SEND);

Uri contentUri = getUriForFile(getApplicationContext(),
"com.example.storage.fileprovider", file); //replace with
                                           package name
intent.setType("text/plain");
intent.putExtra(Intent.EXTRA_STREAM,contentUri);

startActivity(Intent.createChooser(intent , "Sharing Text File"));
```

Assets Folder

The assets folder[18] can be used by application developers for storing arbitrary read-only data prior to compile time, which can be read during runtime. Unlike the res (Resources) folder, any file type can be

---

[18]"App resources overview | Android Developers." 3 Jun. 2019, https://
developer.android.com/guide/topics/resources/providing-resources.
Accessed 11 May. 2020.

stored in this directory; however, it must be added to the application precompilation. To do this, create a folder at the relative file path \app\src\main\assets or in Android Studio via app ➤ New ➤ Folder ➤ Assets Folder. Post compilation, the assets folder is located in the root of the APK under /assets.

Accessing files in the assets folder:

```java
private String readFileFromAssets(String filename, String type)
{
    BufferedReader reader = null;

    StringBuilder stringBuilder = new StringBuilder();

    try {
        reader = new BufferedReader(
                new InputStreamReader(getAssets().
                open(filename), type)); //e.g. "utf-8"

        String mLine;

        while ((mLine = reader.readLine()) != null) {
            stringBuilder.append(mLine+"\n");
        }
    } catch (IOException e) {
        e.printStackTrace();
    } finally {
        if (reader != null) {
            try {
                reader.close();
            } catch (IOException e) {
                e.printStackTrace();
            }
        }
```

```
    }
    return stringBuilder.toString();
}
```

Resources

Similar to assets these resources are read only and are provided precompile time. Unlike the assets folder, data stored in the resource folder (located in the APK root under /res) must follow specific conventions such as file types. Examples of data that can be included in the res folder include XML files for strings and integers as well as application icons.

Return a string (strings should be stored in the strings.xml file) from the res folder:

```
getApplicationContext().getString(R.string.string_name)
```

Return an image from the res folder. Bear in mind that images are stored in the root of the Res drawable folder and that, when accessing an image, to not include the image extension:

```
ContextCompat.getDrawable(getApplicationContext(), R.drawable.image_name)
```

CHAPTER 7

Android Unique Identifiers

Unique identifiers can be used for an array of tasks, from allowing users to set advertising preferences, uniquely identifying a user, and identifying a specific device. There are also strong privacy concerns when it comes to the use of unique identifiers enforced by both Android permissions and the Google Play Developer Policy.

In an attempt to address user privacy concerns, as of Android 10 (API level 29), there has been a large change in how hardware unique identifiers can be accessed from within Android applications. This being that an application must be a device or profile owner, have special carrier permissions, or have the `READ_PRIVILEGED_PHONE_STATE` privileged permission in order to access nonresettable device identifiers. The `READ_PRIVILEGED_PHONE_STATE permission` is only available to applications signed with the device's platform (system application) key[1].

---

[1]"Android security part 1: application signatures & permissions ...." 4 May. 2015, `https://boundarydevices.com/android-security-part-1-application-signatures-permissions/`. Accessed 11 May. 2020.

© James Stevenson 2021
J. Stevenson, *Android Software Internals Quick Reference*,
https://doi.org/10.1007/978-1-4842-6914-5_7

Google Play Advertising ID

As of Android KitKat (API level 4.4), the Google Play Advertising ID[2] can be used to uniquely identify a user of a device. When available on a device, it is an offense against the Google Play Developer Programme Policy to use any other device unique identifiers for advertising purposes. The benefit of the advertising ID for an end user is that it is both resettable and can be used for customizing personalized advertising. An example of the ID returned is a string representation of `9fdbfa02-7f28-422e-944e-f02393a9360e`. As the advertising ID is provided by the Google Play Services API, it means that it will only be available on devices with Google Play Services.

The advertising ID can be used by adding the following library path to the build.gradle file's dependencies tag:

```
implementation 'com.google.android.gms:play-services-ads:7.0.0'
```

*Retrieving the advertising ID (this cannot be done on the main thread - this example uses an AsyncTask; see Chapter **9** for more information):*

```
void getAdvertisingID(final Context context){

    AsyncTask.execute(new Runnable() {
        @Override
        public void run() {
            Info adInfo = null;
            try {
```

---

[2]"Advertising ID - Play Console Help - Google Support." `https://support.google.com/googleplay/android-developer/answer/6048248?hl=en-GB`. Accessed 21 May. 2020.

```
            adInfo = AdvertisingIdClient.getAdvertising
            IdInfo(context);
        } catch (IOException e) {
            e.printStackTrace();
        } catch (GooglePlayServicesNotAvailableException e) {
            e.printStackTrace();
        } catch (GooglePlayServicesRepairableException e) {
            e.printStackTrace();
        }
        String adId = adInfo != null ? adInfo.getId() :
        null;

        Log.v("Advertising ID",adId);

    }
});
}
```

Android ID (Secure Settings Android ID – SSAID)

This is a unique 64-bit number (e.g., ce79870fa5cbfb56) that is Android's preferred approach for identifying a user of a device for activities outside of advertising. This unique identifier is available on all versions of Android, does not require any additional permissions, and is reset as part of a device factory reset.

Accessing the Android ID:

```
Log.v("Android ID",Settings.Secure.getString(this.
getContentResolver(), Settings.Secure.ANDROID_ID));
```

SIM Serial Number

A SIM serial number is used for international identification and is typically broken down into 19 digits[3]. This breaks down to two digits for the Telecom ID, two digits for the country code, two digits for the network code, four digits for the month and year of manufacturing, two digits for the switch configuration code, six digits for the SIM number, and a single check digit.

The SIM serial number is available on Android up to and including Android Pie (API level 28), where it is restricted in Android 10 and above with the READ_PRIVILEGED_PHONE_STATE permission. To use the SIM serial number prior to Android 10 requires the READ_PHONE_STATE runtime permission.

Retrieving the SIM serial number:

```
TelephonyManager telephonyManager = (TelephonyManager)
getApplicationContext().getSystemService(Context.TELEPHONY_
SERVICE);
Log.v("SIM Serial Number", telephonyManager.
getSimSerialNumber());
```

Phone Number

When writing applications for devices that use telephony, the phone number can be used as a unique identifier. This identifier is available on all versions of Android and is tied to the SIM card on the device (if one is present) and requires the READ_PHONE_STATE or READ_PRIVILEGED_PHONE_ STATE permission to access.

---

[3]"Does my SIM card have a serial number? Is it the same as IMEI?." https:// justaskthales.com/us/does-my-sim-card-have-serial-number-it-same-imei/. Accessed 11 May. 2020.

Retrieving the phone number:

```
TelephonyManager telephonyManager = (TelephonyManager)
getApplicationContext().getSystemService(Context.TELEPHONY_
SERVICE);
Log.v("Phone Number", telephonyManager.getLine1Number());
```

IMEI and MEID

To both uniquely identify devices and prevent theft, all mobile devices are designated an IMEI or MEID number. Depending on the network of the device will depend on which identifier the device has. Devices will have an IMEI number if on GSM (Global System for Mobiles) systems and will have a MEID number if on a CDMA (code division multiple access) system. The main difference between the two is that an IMEI is a 14-digit number, while a MEID is a 15-digit number. Similar to other hardware identifiers, both IMEIs and MEIDs are available on devices prior to Android 10 where it can be read if the application has the READ_PHONE_STATE permission. However, as of Android 10, an application requires the READ_PRIVILEGED_PHONE_STATE.

Pre and including Android N (25) access:

```
TelephonyManager telephonyManager = (TelephonyManager)
getApplicationContext().getSystemService(Context.TELEPHONY_
SERVICE);
Log.v("Device ID", telephonyManager.getDeviceId());
```

Post (and including) Android O (26):

```
TelephonyManager telephonyManager = (TelephonyManager)
getApplicationContext().getSystemService(Context.TELEPHONY_
SERVICE);
Log.v("IMEI", telephonyManager.getImei());
Log.v("MEID", telephonyManager.getMeid());
```

CHAPTER 8

Obfuscation and Encryption

Logging

The Log class in Android can be used to create log messages in logcat (accessible via the adb logcat command); these logs come in a handful of different levels, these being

- **Log.wtf** - "What a Terrible Failure" (treated as an extreme ERROR)

- **Log.e** - ERROR

- **Log.w** - WARNING

- **Log.i** - INFO

- **Log.d** - DEBUG

- **Log.v** - VERBOSE

As stated, these log messages can be read via logcat. Logcat is Android's logging system and logs everything from system messages to stack traces. Applications can write to logcat by using the Log class, and in turn these messages can be viewed by using the adb logcat command or in programs such as Android Studio.

© James Stevenson 2021
J. Stevenson, *Android Software Internals Quick Reference*,
https://doi.org/10.1007/978-1-4842-6914-5_8

Irrespective of which of these levels you choose, all log levels will be displayed in logcat. For example, the following logger code, while specifying debug, will be logged to logcat irrespective of the build type (i.e., it will be logged in a release build). It is also worth bearing in mind that the debug log messages will be compiled into release applications. For example, in the following we can see a comparison between a log message in Java and its disassembled release build in Smali (a human-readable representation of Dalvik bytecode).

In Java:

```
Log.d(TAG, "I am a normal debug log message");
```

In Smali:

```
iget-object p1, p0, Lcom/example/logger/MainActivity;-
>TAG:Ljava/lang/String;
```

```
const-string v0, "A log using is loggable"
```

```
invoke-static {p1, v0}, Landroid/util/Log;->d(Ljava/lang/
String;Ljava/lang/String;)I
```

Standard Logging

There are several reasons where a developer may not want to use standard logging. These come down to security and performance, where both a log should be hidden from a malicious actor and a flood of logs should be avoided on an end user's device.

Standard log:

```
Log.d(TAG, "I am a normal debug log Message");
```

Final Constant Variables

One supported way of limiting the amount of log statements in release code is by using the Gradle BuildConfig file which is generated by Gradle prebuild. This file is generated with the following line set to true if building a debug build and false if building a release build.

DEBUG value in BuildConfig file:

```
public static final boolean DEBUG = Boolean.
parseBoolean("true");
```

Implementing the DEBUG constant:

```
if (BuildConfig.DEBUG){
    Log.d(TAG,"This is a log that won't be compiled in a
release build.");
}
```

When building for release, and set to false, the Java compiler will see that it is impossible for the final variable to be true and so doesn't compile the code inside of the if statement. This both means that the log won't be displayed in logcat and also means that the log string won't exist in the application's source code as with a normal log message.

A similar affect to using BuildConfig.DEBUG can also be achieved if not using Gradle. This can be done using a final boolean and setting it to true when debugging and false for the release build.

Setting a custom DEBUG constant:

```
final boolean SHOULD_LOG = false;
if (SHOULD_LOG){
    Log.d(TAG," A log that should never happen...");
}
```

Using .isLoggable

Another way of checking if a log message should be displayed is by using the
.isLoggable method built into the Log class. This method checks the log
level set for the specific tag (the default for an application is INFO). The log
levels work in a hierarchy, as listed at the top of this section. Meaning that
if the log level is set to Verbose, all levels above it will also be true. Unlike
when using BuildConfig, as this value can change programmatically, this
string will be compiled into the application's code base.

Example of Log.isLoggable:

```
if (Log.isLoggable(TAG,Log.DEBUG)){
    Log.d(TAG,"A log using is loggable");
}
```

This log level can be set via the shell using:

```
setprop log.tag.<log_tag> <log_level>
```

Dynamically Checking If Debuggable

The last technique discussed here for limiting the amount of logs written to
logcat is by dynamically checking if an application is in a debug state. Like
the above, as this value can change, the log and string will be compiled
into the built release application.

Example of dynamically checking if an application is in a debug state:

```
boolean isDebuggable =  ( 0 != ( getApplicationInfo().flags &
ApplicationInfo.FLAG_DEBUGGABLE ) );
if (isDebuggable){
    Log.d(TAG,"This log will check programmatically if the app
is debuggable.");
}
```

ProGuard

The most common Android obfuscation tool is ProGuard, with DexGuard[1] being the premium alternative. ProGuard analyzes and optimizes the Java bytecode rather than the direct Java/Kotlin code base. ProGuard implements a collection of techniques[2], these being:

- **Shrinking** - Identifies and removes dead code that is not reachable or is unused. Including classes, fields, methods, and attributes.

- **Optimizer** - Performs optimization on code and code flow where performance changes can be made.

- **Obfuscator** - Renaming aspects of the codebase (i.e., classes, fields, and methods) to names that are deliberately obscure and meaningless.

- **Preverifier** - Performs preverification checks on the bytecode, where if the checks are successful, the classfiles are annotated with preverification information. This is required for Java Micro Edition and for Java 6 and higher.

Enabling ProGuard

Edit the `buildTypes` tag in the `gradle.build` file to `minifyEnabled true`.

For example:

```
buildTypes {
    release {
```

---

[1]"DexGuard vs. ProGuard | Guardsquare." 13 Apr. 2017, `https://www.guardsquare.com/en/blog/dexguard-vs-proguard`. Accessed 12 May. 2020.

[2]"ProGuard manual | Introduction | Guardsquare." `https://www.guardsquare.com/en/products/proguard/manual/introduction`. Accessed 11 May. 2020.

```
    minifyEnabled true
    proguardFiles getDefaultProguardFile('proguard-android-
    optimize.txt'), 'proguard-rules.pro'
  }
}
```

The ProGuard Mapping File

After following the above when making a release build, using Gradle, the Java bytecode will have been analyzed by ProGuard. ProGuard will provide a log file of the stages undergone. This is saved at the following relative path to the application project root.

Mapping file relative location:

```
app/build/outputs/mapping/release/mapping.txt
```

This file shows the changes that ProGuard has implemented. An example of part of this file is below. In this example it can be seen that the function showString in MainActivity has been allow-listed while the other function in *MainActivity* named *loadMe* has not and is now renamed to n.

Example of mapping file:

```
com.example.java_dexloadable.MainActivity -> com.example.java_
dexloadable.MainActivity:
    java.lang.String loadMe() -> n
    1:1:java.lang.String com.example.java_dexloadable.
    StringsClass.stringGetter(int):0:0 -> showString
    1:1:void showString(android.content.Context,int):0 ->
    showString
    2:2:void showString(android.content.Context,int):0:0 ->
    showString
```

If a function or class is not in this mapping, then it has been shrunken out (meaning that it wasn't being used in the code), or it has not been obfuscated (due to being allow-listed).

The ProGuard Allow-List

By default, ProGuard will shrink, optimize, and obfuscate everything in the Java bytecode. This can be controlled by editing the ProGuard file located at app\proguard-rules.pro, in the root of an application directory. This file can be renamed and moved and is specified in the gradle.build file.

The following example rule allow-lists the showString function in the class com.example.java_dexloadable.MainActivity. Here you need to specify the access level of the class and function (public, private, package-private, etc.) as well as the parameters for the function:

```
-keep class com.example.java_dexloadable.MainActivity {
    public showString(android.content.Context, int);
}
```

The following example is the same; however, in this example all functions in the MainActivity are allow-listed:

```
-keep class com.example.java_dexloadable.MainActivity {
    public *;
}
```

The Different Types of Keep

In the preceding two examples, the keep keyword is used. There are several different types of keep[3] keyword. These are summarized in Table 8-1.

Table 8-1. *ProGuard Types of Keep*

	No Rule	-keep	-keepclassmembers	-keepnames
Shrinks Classes	✓	X	✓	✓
Shrinks Members	✓	X	X	✓
Obfuscates Classes	✓	X	✓	X
Obfuscates Members	✓	X	X	X

Entry Points

ProGuard automatically allow-lists (also known as white-lists) entry points to an application (e.g., an activity with the MAIN or LAUNCHER category). It's important to bear in mind that entry points used as part of reflection will not be automatically allow-listed, and so if using refection, these entry points will have to be manually allow-listed. This, however, will minimize the effectiveness of obfuscation as the frequency of plain text components will be higher. The entry points that are automatically added to an allow-list by ProGuard typically include classes with main methods, applets, MIDlets, activities, etc. This also includes classes that have calls to native C code.

---

[3]"Distinguishing between the different ProGuard ... - jebware.com." 14 Nov. 2017, https://jebware.com/blog/?p=418. Accessed 11 May. 2020.

Example Rules

In the following example, the Java Package Name is java_dexloadable, and all rules have been added to the Proguard-rules.pro file.

Keeps (allow-lists) all methods in the MainActivity class:

```
-keep class com.example.java_dexloadable.MainActivity {
    public *;
}
```

Keeps (allow-lists) the showString function in the MainActivity class as well as the MainActivity class itself:

```
-keep class com.example.java_dexloadable.MainActivity {
    public showString(android.content.Context, int);
}
```

Keeps (allow-lists) everything under the top-level package (shouldn't be used):

```
-keep class com.example.java_dexloadable.** { *; }
```

Keeps (allow-lists) the function stringGetter but not the class StringsClass itself:

```
-keepclassmembers class com.example.java_dexloadable.
StringsClass {
    public stringGetter(int);
}
```

Repackage whole package into a single root:

```
-repackageclasses
```

Doesn't perform the ProGuard shrink step:

```
--dontshrink
```

Public Key/Certificate Pinning

Public key pinning allows an application to associate a specific cryptographic public key with a given web server. This in turn is used to decrease the possibility of man in the middle attacks.

When performing public key pinning, the public key of the web server being connected to is required.

There are two fairly simple approaches for doing this – either use the following openssl command, or use the following code and extract the public key from the error message:

```
openssl x509 -in cert.crt -pubkey -noout | openssl
pkey -pubin -outform der | openssl dgst -sha256 -binary |
openssl enc -base64
```

Use the hash of the public key from the preceding message as your hash in the below code. In Android, networking cannot be performed on the main thread, and so it will need to be in a long-running service, an AsyncTask, or thread (detailed in Chapter 9).

Add the following dependency to your build.gradle file as this example uses the OkHTTP library. Also make sure that the application has the Internet permission and that no networking is done on the main thread:

```
implementation("com.squareup.okhttp3:okhttp:4.9.0")
```

Certificate pinning example:

```
String hostname =  "google.com";

CertificatePinner certPinner = new CertificatePinner.Builder()
        .add(
                hostname,
                "sha256/MeCugOOsbHh2GNsYG8FO7wO7E4rjtmR7oo
                LM4iXHJlM="
        )
        .build();

OkHttpClient okHttpClient = new OkHttpClient.Builder()
        .certificatePinner(certPinner)
        .build();

HttpUrl.Builder urlBuilder = HttpUrl.
parse("https://"+hostname).newBuilder();
String url = urlBuilder.build().toString();

MediaType JSON = MediaType.parse("application/json;
charset=utf-8");
RequestBody body = RequestBody.create(JSON,
"{\"test\":\"testvalue\"}");
```

```
Request request = new Request.Builder()
        .url(url)
        .post(body)
        .build();

Log.v(TAG,request.toString());

Response response = null;
try {
    response = okHttpClient.newCall(request).execute();
    ResponseBody jsonData = response.body();
    Log.v(TAG, jsonData.toString());

} catch (IOException e) {
    e.printStackTrace();
}

return Result.success();
```

AES Encryption

AES uses a symmetric algorithm, meaning that the same key is applied for both encryption and decryption. The following is a lightweight example of implementing AES-256 encryption in Java.

The following is an example of an AES-256 encryption approach in Java:

```
try {
    Cipher cipher = null;
    cipher = Cipher.getInstance("AES/CBC/PKCS5PADDING");

    KeyGenerator keygen = null;
    keygen = KeyGenerator.getInstance("AES");
```

```
keygen.init(256);
SecretKey key = keygen.generateKey();

String plainTextString = "I am a plain text";
String cipherTextAsString = "N/A";
String newPlainTextAsString = "N/A";
byte[] plainText = plainTextString.getBytes();

cipher.init(Cipher.ENCRYPT_MODE, key);

byte[] cipherText = new byte[0];

cipherText = cipher.doFinal(plainText);
if (Build.VERSION.SDK_INT >= Build.VERSION_CODES.KITKAT) {
    cipherTextAsString = new String(cipherText,
    StandardCharsets.UTF_8);
}

IvParameterSpec iv = new IvParameterSpec(cipher.getIV());
cipher.init(Cipher.DECRYPT_MODE, key, iv);

byte[] newPlainText = cipher.doFinal(cipherText);
if (Build.VERSION.SDK_INT >= Build.VERSION_CODES.KITKAT) {
    newPlainTextAsString = new String(newPlainText,
    StandardCharsets.UTF_8);
}

if (Build.VERSION.SDK_INT >= Build.VERSION_CODES.O) {
    Log.v(getApplicationContext().getPackageName(), "The
    plaintext '" + plainTextString + "' encrypted is " +
    Base64.getEncoder().encodeToString(cipherText) + " and
    decrypted is '" + newPlainTextAsString);
}
```

```
}catch (NoSuchAlgorithmException e) {
    e.printStackTrace();
} catch (InvalidKeyException e) {
    e.printStackTrace();
} catch (InvalidAlgorithmParameterException e) {
    e.printStackTrace();
} catch (NoSuchPaddingException e) {
    e.printStackTrace();
} catch (BadPaddingException e) {
    e.printStackTrace();
} catch (IllegalBlockSizeException e) {
    e.printStackTrace();
}
```

CHAPTER 9

Services, Launchers, and Components

Long-Running Services

In Android there are several ways that "jobs" can be tasked for a one-off or periodic running after the current activity closes. The techniques discussed here will vary between being the two following types:

- **Strongly bound** to the current activity, such as AsyncTask, meaning that if the activity finishes, then the task is garbage collected.

- **Not strongly bound** to the current activity, such as JobScheduler, where the task continues even after the parent activity itself is garbage collected.

Triggers

Triggers are the mechanism for how a long-running service is tasked and run, these being the initial entry points for the service. Most of these triggers will provide some form of persistence to the service. These triggers can be seen in Table 9-1.

© James Stevenson 2021
J. Stevenson, *Android Software Internals Quick Reference*,
https://doi.org/10.1007/978-1-4842-6914-5_9

Table 9-1. *Long-Running Service Triggers*

Trigger	Description
Intent	Triggered directly and immediately from the code, generally from user interaction.
AlarmManager	Triggered at a specific time in the future, one-off or recurring.
BroadcastReceiver	Triggered when a particular broadcast message is received. For example, `BootComplete`, `PowerConnected`, or custom receivers.
Sensors Callbacks	Triggered when a particular sensor value is received.
WorkManager	Either using `JobScheduler` or `AlarmManager` and `BootComplete` depending on the API level.
JobScheduler	As of API level 21 (Android L), a smarter implementation of an `AlarmManager` allowing for running depending on network, idle, and charging state. Also Doze compliant.

Services

There are several types of "service" that can be run to provide long-running background work to an application. These can be seen in Table 9-2.

Table 9-2. *Long-Running Service Types*

Service	Description
WorkManager	Encapsulating both the launcher and service element (allowing for backward compatibility as the underlying implementation is abstracted). WorkManagers have a minimum period between concurrent work of 15 minutes, and each worker should only run for a maximum of 10 minutes. WorkManagers also automatically persist after a reboot (using a BootComplete broadcast receiver if the permission is available).
JobScheduler	Encapsulating both the launcher and service element. These are highly customizable and can run work depending on environmental factors such as network, idle, and battery state. In addition to this, they can be defined to run at specific intervals or at specific time frames as well as to persist over a reboot (using a BootComplete broadcast receiver if the permission is available). The minimum period between work is 15 minutes.
Service	There are many types of services; however, one of the most common is intent services, where work requests run sequentially. Subsequent requests (intents to the service) wait until the first operation is finished.
Thread	Primarily used for jobs when not wanting to work on the UI thread (such as networking), however, can be used for long-running background work as long as their parent isn't killed. A thread is bound to the parent application.
AsyncTask	Bound to the life of the parent Activity, meaning that if the Activity finishes or is killed, so is the AsyncTask. The advantage here is that it is easier to push work back to the UI thread from an AsyncTask.

(continued)

Table 9-2. (*continued*)

Service	Description
Foreground Service	As of API 26 background services (such as the intent service) are restricted to only running when the application is in the foreground. The replacement for this is foreground services, where when running they must display a constant notification to the user (e.g., a music app showing a music player while playing).

IntentService, AlarmManager, and BootComplete

As noted previously an `IntentService`[1] is a type of service that cannot directly interact with the UI. The work requests in an `IntentService` run sequentially where requests will wait until the current operation is finished. An operation running on an `IntentService` can't be interrupted.

An `AlarmManager`[2] is a mechanism in Android that allows for the delayed and continued running of code in a background thread. An `AlarmManager` can be configured to run at a specific time in the future and at preconfigured intervals. The `AlarmManager` also has a `setAlarmClock` option which allows it to trigger even if the device is in a low-power idle or Doze mode.

---

[1]"Create a background service | Android Developers." `https://developer.android.com/training/run-background-service/create-service`. Accessed 11 May. 2020.

[2]"android.app.AlarmManager - Android Developers." 27 Dec. 2019, `https://developer.android.com/reference/android/app/AlarmManager`. Accessed 11 May. 2020.

A BroadcastReceiver can be set up to listen for the Boot Complete intent[3], as discussed in Chapter 4. This intent is sent once the device starts up after being rebooted. In turn starting the AlarmManager after receiving the BootComplete intent will mean that the background service continues running after the device has been rebooted.

As of Android Oreo 8 (API level 26), Android services can no longer be started from a background process.[4] This means that in Android 8+, JobSchedulers or foreground services should be used. Bear in mind that this functionality , while only applying to applications that target Android 8+, it can be enabled by users in the settings[5] page which also puts many additional constraints on how services run in the background.

The following is a function that will set up an AlarmManager to repeat every x minutes as defined by the waitBeforeRepeatInMinutes parameter:

```
public void startPeriodicWork(long waitBeforeRepeatInMinutes){

    // Construct an intent that will execute the AlarmReceiver
    Intent intent = new Intent(context, AlarmReceiver.class);

    // Create a PendingIntent to be triggered when the alarm goes
        off
    final PendingIntent pIntent = PendingIntent.
    getBroadcast(context, AlarmReceiver.REQUEST_CODE,
            intent, PendingIntent.FLAG_UPDATE_CURRENT);
```

---

[3]"Broadcasts overview | Android Developers." 3 Jun. 2019, https://developer.android.com/guide/components/broadcasts. Accessed 11 May. 2020.

[4]"Android 8.0: java.lang.IllegalStateException: Not allowed to ...." https://stackoverflow.com/questions/46445265/android-8-0-java-lang-illegalstateexception-not-allowed-to-start-service-inten. Accessed 21 May. 2020.

[5]"Background Execution Limits | Android Developers." 13 Feb. 2020, https://developer.android.com/about/versions/oreo/background. Accessed 11 May. 2020.

```
// Setup periodic alarm every every half hour from this point
    onwards
long firstMillis = System.currentTimeMillis();
// alarm is set right away
AlarmManager alarm = (AlarmManager) context.getSystemService
(Context.ALARM_SERVICE);

// First parameter is the type: ELAPSED_REALTIME, ELAPSED_
    REALTIME_WAKEUP, RTC_WAKEUP
// Interval can be INTERVAL_FIFTEEN_MINUTES, INTERVAL_HALF_
    HOUR, INTERVAL_HOUR, INTERVAL_DAY

if (alarm != null) {
    alarm.setInexactRepeating(AlarmManager.RTC_WAKEUP,
    firstMillis,
            waitBeforeRepeatInMinutes * 60 * 1000, pIntent);
}

}
```

Next, create the AlarmManager BroadcastReceiver class. Set the process property in the Android manifest so that it will continue to stay alive if the app has closed[6]. As part of this, add the BroadcastReceiver to the AndroidManifest.xml file.

```
<receiver android:name=".receivers.AlarmReceiver"
    android:process=":remote" />
```

---

[6]"Should I use android: process =":remote" in my receiver ...." https://
stackoverflow.com/questions/4311069/should-i-use-android-process-
remote-in-my-receiver. Accessed 21 May. 2020.

Add the following to AlarmReceiver.java:

```java
public class AlarmReceiver extends BroadcastReceiver {
    public static final int REQUEST_CODE = 12345;

    // Triggered by the Alarm periodically (starts the service
       to run task)
    @Override
    public void onReceive(Context context, Intent intent) {

        int tid = Process.myTid();
        Log.v("TaskScheduler", "Started Alarm Receiver with
        tid "+ tid);

        TaskManager taskManager = new TaskManager(context);
        taskManager.oneOffTask();
    }
}
```

Next, add the BroadcastReceiver for BootComplete. Add the following to the AndroidManifest.xml file:

```xml
<receiver android:name=".receivers.BootReceiver">
    <intent-filter>
        <action android:name="android.intent.action.BOOT_
        COMPLETED" />
    </intent-filter>
</receiver>
```

Then create the BootReceiver.java class:

```java
public class BootReceiver extends BroadcastReceiver {
    @Override
    public void onReceive(Context context, Intent intent) {
```

```
        int tid = Process.myTid();
        Log.v("TaskScheduler", "Started Boot Complete Receiver
        with tid "+ tid);

        TaskManager taskManager = new TaskManager(context);
        taskManager.startPeriodicWork(5);
    }
}
```

Finally create the IntentService; for this make a file called
ServiceManager.java:

```
public class ServiceManager extends IntentService {

    public ServiceManager() {
        super("ServiceTest"); //Used to name the worker thread,
                              important only for debugging.
    }

    @Override
    protected void onHandleIntent(Intent intent) {
        int tid = Process.myTid();
        Log.v("TaskScheduler", "Started Service with
        tid "+ tid);

        String val = intent.getStringExtra("foo");
        //todo Add the work to be performed here.
    }
}
```

Add this service to the AndroidManifest.xml file:

```
<service android:name=".managers.ServiceManager"
    android:exported="false"/>
```

Foreground Services

There are an array of different types of services[7] in Android, from started services (which run in the UI thread) to `IntentService` (which run in their own thread) to bound services (which run as long as there is one activity active that is bound to it).

As of Android 8 Oreo (API 26), there are restrictions on Android applications running background services, unless the app itself is in the foreground. In this case instead of using the `context.startService()` method, the `startForegroundService()` method should be used. After this the service has 5 seconds to display a notification to the user and call the `startForeground(1, notification)` method, which lives for the duration of the service until the `stopForeground(true)` and `stopSelf()` methods are called. A foreground service extends the `Service` class as with any other service and, outside of following the preceding rules and restrictions, acts in the same way.

Code such as the following should be used to identify if a background or foreground service should be used:

```
Intent intent = new Intent(context, ServiceManager.class);
//replace with an appropriate intent
if (Build.VERSION.SDK_INT >= Build.VERSION_CODES.O) {
    context.startForegroundService(intent);
}else{
    context.startService(intent);
}
```

---

[7]"Services overview | Android Developers." 3 Jun. 2019, `https://developer.android.com/guide/components/services`. Accessed 11 May. 2020.

As a notification is required as part of the starting of a foreground service, it means that a by-product of this is to set up a notification channel[8] (when targeting Android 8.0 - API level 26 and above). Notification channels were added as a way of providing fine-grained access for end users allowing them to change notification settings and decide which notification channels from an app should be visible.

The following shows an example of setting up a notification channel:

```java
public static void createNotificationChannel(Context context) {

    if (Build.VERSION.SDK_INT >= Build.VERSION_CODES.O) {
        int importance = NotificationManager.IMPORTANCE_
        DEFAULT;
        NotificationChannel channel = new Notification
        Channel(CHANNEL_ID, CHANNEL_NAME, importance);
        channel.setDescription(CHANNEL_DESC);

        NotificationManager notificationManager = context.get
        SystemService(NotificationManager.class);
        if (notificationManager != null) {
            notificationManager.createNotificationChannel
            (channel);
        }
    }
}
```

---

[8]"Create and Manage Notification Channels ...." https://developer.android.com/training/notify-user/channels. Accessed 11 May. 2020.

Sending a notification:

```
Intent notificationIntent = new Intent(this, MainActivity.class);
PendingIntent pendingIntent = PendingIntent.getActivity(this,
        0, notificationIntent, 0);

Notification notification = new NotificationCompat.Builder
(getApplicationContext(), CHANNEL_ID)
        .setContentTitle("Notification Title")
        .setContentText("Notification Text")
        .setSmallIcon(R.mipmap.ic_launcher)
        .setContentIntent(pendingIntent)
        .build();

startForeground(1, notification);
}
```

As of Android 9 (API level 28), in addition to adding your Service to the Android manifest as follows, you will also need to add the FOREGROUND_SERVICE permission:

```
<service android:name=".managers.ForegroundServiceManager"
    android:exported="false"/>
<uses-permission android:name="android.permission.FOREGROUND_
SERVICE" />
```

JobScheduler

As of Android 5 L (API 21), job schedulers have been introduced as a way to task batch jobs for when the device has more resources available. As a whole, multiple pieces of work can be tasked by JobSchedulers, and they will bucket these tasks into batches. It means that the tasked work may not exactly execute when expected; however, it will occur around that time (e.g., a task instructed to execute every 15 minutes may execute after 14 minutes for one run and after 16 minutes for another run).

One of the most powerful features of JobSchedulers is that they allow for the deference of work if specific criteria are or are not set, for example, no network connectivity, the battery is charging, or the device is in an idle state. There is also the option with setPeriodic and setPersisted to run periodic work and for it to persist over a reboot (if the application holds the RECEIVE_BOOT_COMPLETED permission). The setOverrideDeadline option also allows for when running one-off work for a maximum time to allow a wait before forcing the running of the work.

Add the following. If not wanting a periodic worker, then remove the setPeriodic and setPersisted tags:

```
@RequiresApi(api = Build.VERSION_CODES.LOLLIPOP)
public void startJobScheduler(){
    ComponentName serviceComponent = new ComponentName(context,
    JobSchedulerManager.class);
    JobInfo.Builder builder = new JobInfo.Builder
    (0, serviceComponent);
    //builder.setMinimumLatency(1 * 1000); // wait at least /
    Can't call setMinimumLatency() on a periodic job/
    //builder.setOverrideDeadline(3 * 1000); // maximum delay
    //Can't call setOverrideDeadline() on a periodic job.
    builder.setPeriodic(1000); //runs over time
    builder.setPersisted(true); // persists over reboot
    //builder.setRequiredNetworkType(JobInfo.NETWORK_TYPE_
    UNMETERED); // require unmetered network
    //builder.setRequiresDeviceIdle(true); // device should
                                        be idle
    //builder.setRequiresCharging(false);
    // we don't care if the device is charging or not
    JobScheduler jobScheduler = (JobScheduler) context.
    getSystemService(Context.JOB_SCHEDULER_SERVICE);
```

```
    if (jobScheduler != null) {
        jobScheduler.schedule(builder.build());
    }
}
```

Then make a class called JobSchedulerManager.java:

```
@RequiresApi(api = Build.VERSION_CODES.LOLLIPOP)
public class JobSchedulerManager extends JobService {

    @Override
    public boolean onStartJob(JobParameters jobParameters) {

        int tid = Process.myTid();
        Log.v("TaskScheduler", "Started Job Scheduler with tid
        "+ tid);

        //todo perform work here

        // returning false means the work has been done, return
            true if the job is being run asynchronously
        return true;
    }

    @Override
    public boolean onStopJob(JobParameters params) {
        return false;
    }
}
```

Add the following class to the AndroidManifest.xml file:

```
<service android:name=".managers.JobSchedulerManager"
    android:permission="android.permission.BIND_JOB_SERVICE"/>
```

A `JobScheduler` service must be protected with the preceding permission which makes it so that only applications with this permission can task the service. If a job service is declared in the manifest but not protected with this permission, the service will be ignored by the system.

Work Managers

As described in the Android documentation,[9] `WorkManagers` are backward compatible from API 14 onward. A combination of `BroadcastReceiver` and `AlarmManager` is used on API 14-22, and `JobScheduler` is used on API 23+. One of the main disadvantages for using a `WorkManager` instead of an `AlarmManager` is that there are restrictions on their runtime (which is inherited from using a `JobScheduler` behind the scenes); this includes that a `WorkManager` should not run for longer than 10 minutes and cannot perform another piece of consecutive work until a minimum of 15 minutes has passed since the current one started. The reason for this is to comply with the Doze restrictions.

Add the following dependencies to the `gradle.build` file when using work managers:

```
def work_version = "2.3.3"

    // (Java only)
    implementation "androidx.work:work-runtime:$work_version"

    // Kotlin + coroutines
    implementation "androidx.work:work-runtime-ktx:$work_version"
```

---

[9]"Schedule tasks with WorkManager | Android Developers." `https://developer.android.com/topic/libraries/architecture/workmanager`. Accessed 11 May. 2020.

The following code tasks and starts a work manager:

```
PeriodicWorkRequest work = new PeriodicWorkRequest.Builder(
        com.example.taskscheduler.managers.WorkManager.class,
        15, TimeUnit.MINUTES)
        .build(); //update path to match your created
        WorkManager.java class

WorkManager.getInstance().cancelAllWork();
WorkManager.getInstance().enqueue(work);
```

Finally create a class called WorkManager.java:

```
public class WorkManager extends Worker {

    Context context;

    public WorkManager(@NonNull Context context, @NonNull
    WorkerParameters workerParams) {
        super(context, workerParams);

        this.context = context;
    }

    @Override
    public Result doWork() {
        int tid = Process.myTid();
        Log.v("TaskScheduler", "Worker started with tid "+ tid);
        // Todo run your work here.
        return Result.success();
    }
}
```

Threading

Outside of the main application thread (which is created for each application by the system), an application can have multiple additional threads of execution. Threads are fairly simple to set up, however, as with AsyncTasks are bound to the life of their parent (commonly an Activity). This being the case, if a thread's parent is destroyed (i.e., removed from the task stack by the user), then the thread is subject to garbage collection (where unused resources are removed to recover memory for other components).

Starting the thread:

```
public void startThread(){
    Thread thread = new ThreadManager();
    thread.start();
}
```

Make a java class called ThreadManager.java:

```
public class ThreadManager extends Thread{
    public ThreadManager() {
        super();
    }

    @Override
    public void run() {
        long tid = getId();

        // Todo do work here.
        Log.v("TaskScheduler", "Starting a new thread "+ tid);

        while (true){
            Log.v("TaskScheduler", "In a thread: " + tid);
```

```
        try {
            Thread.sleep(1000);
        } catch (InterruptedException e) {
            e.printStackTrace();
        }
    }
  }
}
```

AsyncTasks

Deprecated in Android R – API level 30 (it is instead recommended to use the standard `java.util.concurrent` or Kotlin concurrency utilities instead) – AsyncTasks allow for short running (intended for only a handful of seconds at a time) code on a separate thread while also having access to the UI thread. When constructing an `AsyncTask` object, three types need to be provided; these are:

- The type of the parameters that are passed into the AsyncTask's execution

- The type of the progress units used during background computation

- The type of the result of the background method

AsyncTasks must be loaded, created, and executed on the main thread - as of API level 16, this is done automatically.

Calling an AsyncTasks:

```
AsyncTask<String, Void, Void> task = new myAsyncTask
(getApplicationContext()).execute("example string");
```

Cancelling an AsyncTask:

```
task.cancel(true);
```

Creating an AsyncTask class (make as a private or package-private subclass of your activity class):

```
class myAsyncTask extends AsyncTask<String, Void, Void> {
    private Context mContext;

    public myAsyncTask(Context context) {
        this.mContext = context;
    }

    @Override
    protected Void doInBackground(final String... strings) {
        final Context context = this.mContext;

        runOnUiThread(new Runnable() {
            @Override
            public void run() {
                for (String text:strings) {

                    Toast.makeText(context, text, Toast.LENGTH_
                    SHORT).show();
                }
            }
        });

        return null;
    }
}
```

Battery and Security Effects on Long-Running Services

Long-running services can provide a myriad of useful functionality to users; however, due to battery and security concerns, there are a myriad of ways that long-running services can be killed prematurely. This does vary from service type to service type; however, it will normally be caused by power management restrictions.[10] These include the following runtime restrictions in place:

- Doze mode[11]

- App standby buckets[12]

- App background restrictions

- App battery optimization

Doze

Introduced in Android 6 (API level 23), Doze functions as a battery saver utility by bucketing app runtimes into maintenance windows when the device is idle (meaning that the device has not recently received user interaction for a time). These windows, where applications can run background tasks start frequent, however, over time become more and more disparate the longer the device is idle. This means that while an `AlarmManager` may be tasked to run every 5 minutes, Doze restrictions would apply to stop it from doing so as regularly.

---

[10]"Power management restrictions | Android Developers." 3 Jun. 2018, `https://developer.android.com/topic/performance/power/power-details`. Accessed 11 May. 2020.

[11]"Optimize for Doze and App Standby ...." `https://developer.android.com/training/monitoring-device-state/doze-standby`. Accessed 11 May. 2020.

[12]"App Standby Buckets | Android Developers." 3 Jun. 2018, `https://developer.android.com/topic/performance/appstandby`. Accessed 11 May. 2020.

Alarm manager's restrictions:

- `setExact()` and `setWindow()` alarm manager alarms are deferred to the next maintenance window.

- `setAndAllowWhileIdle()` and `setExactAndAllowWhileIdle()` will start normally during a Doze maintenance window. `setAlarmClock()` will also start during a maintenance window with the system exiting Doze shortly before the alarm fires.

Job scheduler's restrictions:

- JobSchedulers or WorkManagers are suspended.

Miscellaneous restrictions:

- Network access, wake locks, Wi-Fi scans, and sync adapters are ignored and suspended.

You can test how an application runs in Doze mode (on API level 23+) with the following command:

```
adb shell dumpsys deviceidle force-idle
```

Exiting the idle mode can be done by running the following command:

```
adb shell dumpsys deviceidle unforce
```

App Standby Buckets

Android 9 (API level 28) adds another battery-saving feature. This feature assigns all applications into one of four buckets. Each manufacturer can set their own criteria for how an application can be placed in each bucket (the Android documentation highlights that "machine learning" techniques can be used to support this decision process). In turn the exact rationale for why applications are assigned specific buckets is unknown.

These buckets are

- **Active** - The app is currently being used or was very recently used, including if the app has launched an activity or is running a foreground service or the user has clicked on a notification from the app:

    - **Jobs** - No restriction

    - **Alarms** - No restriction

- **Working set** - The app is in regular use:

    - **Jobs** - Deferred up to 2 hours

    - **Alarms** - Deferred up to 6 minutes

- **Frequent** - The app is often used, but not every day:

    - **Jobs** - Deferred up to 8 hours

    - **Alarms** - Deferred up to 30 minutes

- **Rare** - The app is not frequently used:

    - **Jobs** - Deferred up to 24 hours

    - **Alarms** - Deferred up to 2 hours

    - **Networking** - Deferred up to 24 hours

- **Never** - Application is installed but has never been run:

    - Components are disabled if an application has never run.

Modifying a Component's State

Application components are written in the `AndroidManifest.xml file`. As mentioned previously, there are four main types of components, these being

- Activities

- Services

- Broadcast receivers

- Content providers

Statically Modifying Component State

A component can be statically modified by editing its entry's `android:enabled="false"` tag in the Android manifest. The following activity `SecondaryActivity` has been disabled by default via its entry in the Android manifest.

Setting a component's enabled property:

```
<activity android:name=".SecondaryActivity"
    android:enabled="false"
 />
```

Dynamically Modifying Components

There are three main states that components can be set to programmatically, these being

- COMPONENT_ENABLED_STATE_DEFAULT
  - Sets a component to its default state as defined in the manifest.

- COMPONENT_ENABLED_STATE_ENABLED

    - Explicitly enables the component.

- COMPONENT_ENABLED_STATE_DISABLED

    - Explicitly disables the component. A disabled component cannot be used or started.

There are two other component states; however, these cannot be set with the setComponentEnabledSetting method. These are

- COMPONENT_ENABLED_STATE_DISABLED_USER

    - Explicitly disables the component and can be reenabled by the user in the appropriate system UI.

- COMPONENT_ENABLED_STATE_DISABLED_UNTIL_USED

    - This state means that the component should be identified as disabled (i.e., an activity not showing in the launcher) until the user explicitly attempts to use it where it should be set to enabled.

Enabling a component:

```
PackageManager packageManager = getApplicationContext().
getPackageManager();
ComponentName componentName = new ComponentName(getApplication
Context(), SecondaryActivity.class);

packageManager.setComponentEnabledSetting(componentName,
PackageManager.COMPONENT_ENABLED_STATE_ENABLED,PackageManager.
DONT_KILL_APP);
```

Returning the state of a component:

```
PackageManager packageManager = getApplicationContext().
getPackageManager();
ComponentName componentName = new ComponentName(getApplication
Context(), SecondaryActivity.class);

int componentState = packageManager.getComponentEnabledSetting
(componentName);
```

Disabling a component:

```
PackageManager packageManager = getApplicationContext().
getPackageManager();
ComponentName componentName = new ComponentName(getApplication
Context(), SecondaryActivity.class);
packageManager.setComponentEnabledSetting(componentName,
PackageManager.COMPONENT_ENABLED_STATE_DISABLED,PackageManager.
DONT_KILL_APP);
```

Creating an Android Launcher

Implemented in API level 1, the Android Launcher is a component of
Android which allows an Android application to function as the base
activity on the home screen of an Android device (as seen in Figure 9-2).
These home screens can be set by the individual OEMs; however, other
famous launchers include Facebook Home. A launcher must be set in the
settings menu of the Android device as seen in Figure 9-1.

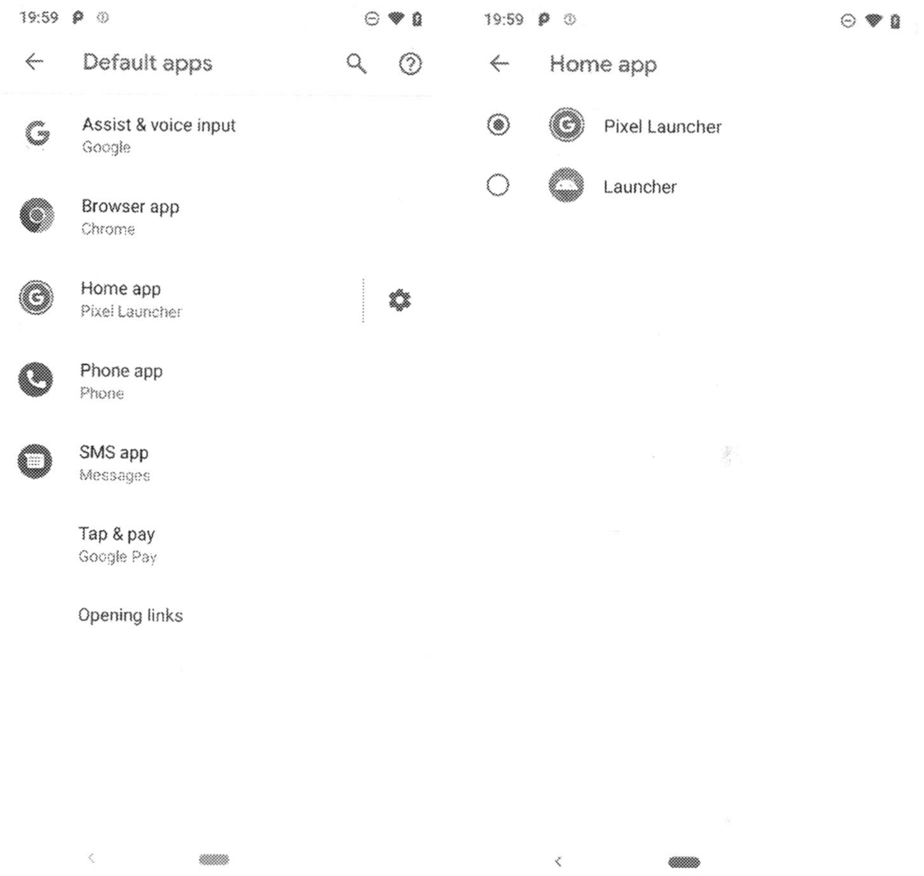

19:59

←   Default apps   Q   ⑦

G   **Assist & voice input**
Google

    Browser app
Chrome

    Home app
Pixel Launcher

    Phone app
Phone

    SMS app
Messages

    Tap & pay
Google Pay

    Opening links

19:59

←   Home app

◉   G   Pixel Launcher

○   Launcher

⚙

Figure 9-1. *Launcher settings*

Figure 9-2. Example launcher

Creating a Launcher Application

First add the following attribute to the activities activity tag in the
AndroidManifest.xml file:

```
android:launchMode="singleTask"
```

Then add two categories to the intent filter of the same activity tag:

```
<category android:name="android.intent.category.DEFAULT" />
<category android:name="android.intent.category.HOME" />
```

At this stage the application will function as a launcher and will be selectable as a home screen from the Android device's settings. The following details several additional techniques that can be useful when creating a launcher.

Additional Functionality

Retrieving a list of applications:

```
private List<ResolveInfo> getListOfApplications(Context
context){
    Intent mainIntent = new Intent(Intent.ACTION_MAIN, null);
    mainIntent.addCategory(Intent.CATEGORY_LAUNCHER);
    List<ResolveInfo> pkgAppsList = context.
    getPackageManager().queryIntentActivities( mainIntent, 0);
    return pkgAppsList;
}
```

Retrieving an application's icon:

```
public static Drawable getActivityIcon(Context context, String
packageName, String activityName) {
    PackageManager pm = context.getPackageManager();
    Intent intent = new Intent();
    intent.setComponent(new ComponentName(packageName,
    activityName));
    ResolveInfo resolveInfo = pm.resolveActivity(intent, 0);

    return resolveInfo.loadIcon(pm);
}
```

Setting an image view. Add an ImageView object to your activity with the name imageView:

```
<ImageView
    android:id="@+id/imageView"
    android:layout_width="129dp"
    android:layout_height="129dp"
    android:foregroundGravity="center_vertical"
    app:srcCompat="@android:drawable/ic_dialog_alert"
    android:layout_gravity="center"
    />
```

Create an on-click listener for the ImageView:

```
ImageView chromeIcon = (ImageView) findViewById(R.
id.imageView);
chromeIcon.setImageDrawable(getActivityIcon(getApplication
Context(),"com.android.chrome", "com.google.android.apps.
chrome.Main"));

ImageView img = findViewById(R.id.imageView);
img.setOnClickListener(new View.OnClickListener() {
    @Override
    public void onClick(View view) {

        Intent launchIntent = getPackageManager().
        getLaunchIntentForPackage("com.android.chrome");
        startActivity(launchIntent);
    }
});
```

Setting the wallpaper. Add the following to the styles.xml in the style tag under the name AppTheme:

```
<item name="android:windowShowWallpaper">true</item>
<item name="android:windowBackground">@android:color/
transparent</item>
```

Hiding the system UI:

```
private void hideSystemUI() {
    View decorView = getWindow().getDecorView();
    decorView.setSystemUiVisibility(
            View.SYSTEM_UI_FLAG_IMMERSIVE
                    | View.SYSTEM_UI_FLAG_LAYOUT_STABLE
                    | View.SYSTEM_UI_FLAG_LAYOUT_HIDE_
                      NAVIGATION
                    | View.SYSTEM_UI_FLAG_LAYOUT_FULLSCREEN
                    | View.SYSTEM_UI_FLAG_HIDE_NAVIGATION
                    | View.SYSTEM_UI_FLAG_FULLSCREEN);
```

CHAPTER 10

Reflection and Class Loading

Reflection

Reflection is one of the many aces up the sleeve when it comes to taking apart Android applications and getting them running in a state that suits you. To put it simply reflection is an API that can be used to access, examine, and modify objects at runtime - this includes fields, methods, classes, and interfaces (as can be seen in Figure 10-1).

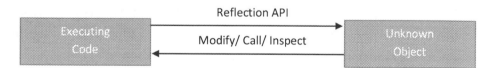

Figure 10-1. *Java reflection diagram*

A summary of these components is listed here:

- **Class** - A class is a blueprint/template where when used individual objects can be created from them. For example, a `Computer` class can be created with an `installedRam` variable, `getRAM()` method, and

setRAM() method. An object can be made using this
class with, for example, Computer myComputer =
new Computer(); then the method setRAM() can be
used on the myComputer object such as myComputer.
setRAM(32);.

- **Method** - A method is a segment of code, with a
specific purpose, which is run when called and can be
part of a class or standalone. Methods can be passed a
series of typed parameters and may return a variable
of a specified type. When made as part of a class, a
method can be static or instance. An instance method
requires an object of its class to be created before it
can be used, while a static method does not rely on an
initialized object. For example, the class Computer may
have a sum static method that adds two numbers and
returns the result, and a setRAM() instance method
which sets the ram variable for the specific instance of
the created object.

- **Constructor** - A constructor is a special type of method
that is used as part of the initialization of an object (e.g.,
a class) to set variables and call methods. For example,
the House class may have a constructor method
which takes three variables as parameters: hight,
numberOfRooms, and hasGarden. Then a House object
can be created with House myHouse = new House(10,
2, false);.

- **Interface** - An interface is an abstract class that
contains a collection of methods with empty bodies.
For example, having a Creature interface may have

methods such as move(), speak(), and eat() of which
all would need to be populated depending on the class
(type of creature) that implemented the interface.

In the following examples, two classes will be used to help display an
array of different reflection techniques. If not using these example classes,
replace the applicable references in the code samples:

A helper class to demonstrate reflection:

```
public class Loadable {
    private final static String description = "This is a class
    that contains an assortment of access modifiers to test
    different types of reflection.";
    private Context context;
    private long uniqueId = 0;
    private long time = 0;
    private DeviceData deviceData = new DeviceData();

    public void setDeviceInfo() {
        deviceData.setDeviceInfo();
    }

    public long getTime() {
        return time;
    }

    private Loadable(Context context, long uniqueId) {
        this.context = context;
        this.uniqueId = uniqueId;
    }

    private void setTime(){
        this.time = System.currentTimeMillis();
    }
}
```

```
    private static String getDeviceName(){
        return android.os.Build.MODEL;
    }

    protected static Loadable construct(Context context){

        final int uniqueId = new Random().nextInt((1000) + 1);

        Loadable loadable = new Loadable(context, uniqueId);
        loadable.setDeviceInfo();
        return loadable;

    }
}
```

Helper class to support presenting an array of functionality when loading:

```
public class DeviceData {

    String version = "";  // OS version
    String sdkLevel = ""; // API Level
    String device = "";   // Device
    String model = "";    // Model
    String product = ""; // Product

    public void setDeviceInfo(){
        version = System.getProperty("os.version");
        sdkLevel = android.os.Build.VERSION.SDK;
        device = android.os.Build.DEVICE;
        model = android.os.Build.MODEL;
        product = android.os.Build.PRODUCT;
    }
```

```
    @Override
    public String toString() {
        return "DeviceData{" +
                "version='" + version + '\'' +
                ", sdkLevel='" + sdkLevel + '\'' +
                ", device='" + device + '\'' +
                ", model='" + model + '\'' +
                ", product='" + product + '\'' +
                '}';
    }
}
```

Making an Instance of a Class

In the following example, using reflection, a new instance of the
DeviceData class is created, and a call to the setDeviceInfo method (to
populate its fields) is run before logging the initialized state of one of those
fields.

Initializing a class:

```
try {
    Object initialisedDeviceData= DeviceData.class.
    newInstance();
    initialisedDeviceData.getClass().getDeclaredMethod
    ("setDeviceInfo").invoke(initialisedDeviceData);
    String model = (String) initialisedDeviceData.getClass().
    getDeclaredField("model").get(initialisedDeviceData);
    Log.v(TAG, model);

} catch (IllegalAccessException e) {
    e.printStackTrace();
} catch (InstantiationException e) {
```

```
    e.printStackTrace();
} catch (NoSuchMethodException e) {
    e.printStackTrace();
} catch (InvocationTargetException e) {
    e.printStackTrace();
} catch (NoSuchFieldException e) {
    e.printStackTrace();
}
```

.getDeclaredMethod Compared With .getMethod

In the following example, we see the differences between the methods getMethods and getDeclaredMethods - this is also the same for getFields and getDeclaredFields. getMethods will return an array containing public methods of the class or interface as well as any inherited from superclasses or superinterfaces (a superclass/superinterface is an object from which multiple subobjects can be created). getDeclaredMethods on the other hand returns all of the declared methods (not just public) of the class or interface.

The main difference here is that if needing to access a private method, the getDeclaredMethods method will be used, and then the accessibility will be set with the .setAccessible method, whereas if needing to access methods of the superclasses or superinterfaces, getMethods will be used instead.

getMethods() example:

```
for (Method method : Loadable.class.getMethods()){
    Log.v(TAG, method.getName());
 }
```

getDeclaredMethods() example:

```
for (Method method : Loadable.class.getDeclaredMethods()){
    method.setAccessible(true);
    Log.v(TAG, method.getName());
 }
```

Static Methods

In the case of static methods, an instance of a class is not needed to use reflection.

Static method example:

```
try {
    Method getDeviceName = Loadable.class.getDeclaredMethod
    ("getDeviceName");
    getDeviceName.setAccessible(true);
    Log.v(TAG,(String) getDeviceName.invoke(Loadable.class));
} catch (NoSuchMethodException e) {
    e.printStackTrace();
} catch (IllegalAccessException e) {
    e.printStackTrace();
} catch (InvocationTargetException e) {
    e.printStackTrace();
}
```

Private Constructors

In the case where a class' constructor is private, reflection can still be used to construct the class and access its fields and methods.

An additional quirk when talking about constructors is that when a member variable is defined in a class – such as `String myMemberVariable = android.os.Build.VERSION.SDK;` – this is moved to the constructor of the class by the compiler.[1]

The following is an example of constructing a class with a private constructor:

```
try {
    Constructor<?> constructor = Loadable.class.getDeclared
    Constructor(Context.class, long.class);
    constructor.setAccessible(true);
    Object instance = constructor.newInstance(getApplication
    Context(), (Object) 12); // constructor takes a context and
                            an id.
    Field uniqueIdField = instance.getClass().getDeclared
    Field("uniqueId");
    uniqueIdField.setAccessible(true);
    long uniqueId = (long) uniqueIdField.get(instance);
    Log.v(TAG, ""+uniqueId);

} catch (InstantiationException e) {
    e.printStackTrace();
} catch (InvocationTargetException e) {
    e.printStackTrace();
} catch (NoSuchMethodException e) {
    e.printStackTrace();
```

---

[1]"Should I use android: process =":remote" in my receiver ...." `https://stackoverflow.com/questions/4311069/should-i-use-android-process-remote-in-my-receiver`. Accessed 21 May. 2020.

```
} catch (IllegalAccessException e) {
    e.printStackTrace();
} catch (NoSuchFieldException e) {
    e.printStackTrace();
}
```

Initialized Classes as Fields of Other Classes

The following example uses reflection twice: first to initialize a class and gain access to one of its fields and secondly to use reflection on that field (which is a class of its own) to access one of its fields (which is a string).

Instance class example:

```
try {
    // The loadable class has a static method that can be
        used to construct it in this example, however, if the
        constructor isn't public,
    // this can also be done with the private constructor
        example.
    // and can be done as in the public class example.
    Object instance = Loadable.class.getDeclared
    Method("construct", Context.class)
            .invoke(Loadable.class, getApplicationContext());

    // Retrieve the field device data which is the class we're
    looking to get the data of.
    Field devicdDataField = instance.getClass().getDeclared
    Field("deviceData");
    devicdDataField.setAccessible(true);
    Object initialisedDeviceData = devicdDataField.
    get(instance);
```

```
    // After accessing the value from the field we're looking
        to access the filds of we can use the same type of
        reflection again after getting it's class.
    Field modelField = initialisedDeviceData.getClass().
    getDeclaredField("device");
    modelField.setAccessible(true);
    String model = (String) modelField.get(initialised
    DeviceData);

    Log.v(TAG,model);

} catch (IllegalAccessException e) {
    e.printStackTrace();
} catch (InvocationTargetException e) {
    e.printStackTrace();
} catch (NoSuchMethodException e) {
    e.printStackTrace();
} catch (NoSuchFieldException e) {
    e.printStackTrace();
}
```

Class Loading

Java Class Loaders[2] are a component of the Java Runtime Environment
(JRE) which load Java classes into a Java Virtual Machine (JVM)/Dalvik
Virtual Machine (DVM)/Android Runtime (ART). Not all classes are loaded
simultaneously, nor with the same ClassLoader. The context method
getClassLoader() can be used to get the current class loader. There are
several types of class loading in Android, these being:

---

[2]"Catherine22/ClassLoader: Loading apks or classes ... - GitHub." https://
github.com/Catherine22/ClassLoader. Accessed 16 May. 2020.

- **PathClassLoader** - This is used by the Android system for its system and application class loader(s).

- **DexClassLoader** - This loads file types containing a .dex file (e.g., .jar and .apk or .dex file directly). These .dex files (Dalvik executable) contain Dalvik bytecode.

- **URLClassLoader** - This is used to retrieve classes or resources via URL paths. Paths ending with / are assumed to be directories, while otherwise they are assumed to be .jar files.

The following performs class loading using a Dalvik executable and DexClassLoader.

Retrieve the current class loader:

```
ClassLoader loader = getApplicationContext().getClassLoader();
```

As of API level 26 (Android O), it is possible to read a dex file directly from memory. To do this, read a ByteBuffer of a file, and use the class InMemoryDexClassLoader. The following is a helper function for reading a file to a byte array:

```
private static byte[] readFileToByteArray(File file){
    FileInputStream fis = null;

    byte[] bArray = new byte[(int) file.length()];
    try{
        fis = new FileInputStream(file);
        fis.read(bArray);
        fis.close();

    }catch(IOException ioExp){
        ioExp.printStackTrace();
    }
    return bArray;
}
```

In memory dex class loading:

```
dexLoader = new InMemoryDexClassLoader(ByteBuffer.wrap(readFile
ToByteArray(filePath)), loader);
```

The other option is to load the dex file directly from the file. The DexClassLoader class takes the dexPath (file path) of the .dex file, the optimizedDirectory - where .odex (optimized dex files) are stored prior to Android API level 26, the librarySearchPath - a string list (delimited by File.pathSeparator;) stating directories containing native libraries, and parent - the parent ClassLoader.

```
dexLoader = new DexClassLoader(filePath, dexCacheDirectory.
getAbsolutePath(), null, loader);
```

After creating a dex class loader, choose the class to load, as a string:

```
loadedClass = dexLoader.loadClass("me.jamesstevenson.
dexloadable.MainActivity"); //alter path for your use case
```

At this stage the uninitialized class can be used as normal, as described in the reflection section. The following shows how to safely initialize this class:

```
initialisedClass = loadedClass != null ? loadedClass.
newInstance() : null;
```

After initializing this class, a specific method can be called, as a string, and its response can be returned as done previously with standard reflection:

```
method = loadedClass != null ? loadedClass.getMethod("loadMeAnd
IllTakeContext", Context.class) : null;
Object methodResponse = method != null ? method.
invoke(initialisedClass, getApplicationContext()) : null;
```

CHAPTER 11

The Android Shell

Android is built upon Linux meaning that when using adb (Android's proprietary command-line tool that allows for communication with a device), you can issue common Linux commands (such as *ls*, *cd*, *whoami*, etc.) as well as several commands unique to the Android operating system.

The following are several examples of basic device input via the shell:

```
input text "Hello World"
input swipe 50 050 450 100 #coordinates for swipe action
input tap 466 17 #coordinates for tap
service call phone 1 s16 098765432
service call statusbar 1
service call statusbar 2
```

Requiring root the following displays the boot image above all other activities. This does not stop activities from running in the foreground behind the animation.

```
/system/bin/bootanimation
```

© James Stevenson 2021
J. Stevenson, *Android Software Internals Quick Reference*,
https://doi.org/10.1007/978-1-4842-6914-5_11

Control system properties via the svc command (requires root):

```
svc -l
svc bluetooth enable/ disable
svc wifi enable/ disable
svc nfc enable/ disable
svc data enable/ disable
svc power reboot
svc power shutdown
svc power stayon true #[true|false|usb|ac|wireless]
svc usb getFunctions [function] #Possible values of [function]
are any of 'mtp', 'ptp', 'rndis', 'midi'
```

The screencap command takes a photo of the screen and saves it to a location on device. Similarly, the screenrecord command records the screen for a maximum of 3 minutes and saves it to disk:

```
screencap -p /sdcard/screen.png
screenrecord /sdcard/MyVideo.mp4
```

List all running processes:

```
top
top | grep chrome
```

Install an application on the device, which requires root. The -g permission accepts all runtime permission without user interaction (this option didn't exist prior to Android 6.0 as neither did runtime permissions).

```
pm install -g /data/local/tmp/one.apk
```

Return a list of the input devices available on the device. This can include audio buttons, power button, touch screen, fingerprint reader, and a mouse.

```
uinput-fpc - Finger print sensor
fts - screen
gpio-keys - volume button
qpnp_pon - volume / power buttons
ls /dev/input/ -l
lsof | grep input/event
# or get the name of the inputs and see when an event occurs on
that input
getevent -l
# Return feedback if an input is in use. Useful for identifying
if the screen is in use.
cat /dev/input/event2
# Send an event to one of these inputs. For example on my
device the below sets the volume to 0.
sendevent /dev/input/event0 0 0 0
```

Start an application via the Monkey testing tool (a UI fuzzer). Replace the number 1 with the number of random touch inputs to perform as part of the test:

```
monkey -p com.android.chrome 1
```

If you know the activity name, you can start the application with activity manager instead:

```
am start -n com.android.chrome/com.google.android.apps.chrome.
Main
```

The following returns the manufacturer, device name, version, name and date, as well as user and release keys:

```
getprop ro.build.fingerprint # i.e. google/blueline/blueline:9/
PQ3A.190605.003/5524043:user/release-keys
# Returns the kernel version
uname -a
# Also returns the kernel version as well as the device
architecture.
cat /proc/version
```

Access an application's internal storage (requires root):

```
#As Root access the locations used by applications as their
internal storage.
cd /data/user/0
# For example accessing the saved offline pages in Chrome and
storing it in the data/local/tmp directory for it to be pulled
off device later.
su
cd /data/user/0
cd com.android.chrome/cache/Offline Pages/archives
cp 91-a05c-b3f3384516f4.mhtml /data/local/tmp/page.mhtml
chmod 777 /data/local/tmp/page.mhtml
```

Reboot the device. An application requires the android.permission. REBOOT permission or to be root:

```
/system/bin/reboot
reboot
svc power reboot
svc power shutdown
```

As root mount a file system as read-write. On older devices this can be used for setting the system apps directory to read-write.

```
busybox mount -o remount,rw /system
```

Interrupts allow interface devices to communicate with the processors:

```
cat /proc/interrupts | grep volume
```

Dumpsys provides information on system services:

```
dumpsys -l
dumpsys input
dumpsys meminfo
service call procstats 1
```

Running Commands Programmatically

Using the runtime class, shell commands can be run programmatically. Commands will fail if they require a higher permission level than the application possesses – for example, attempting to reboot a device without the *android.permission.REBOOT permission.*

Run a single command:

```
String filesLocation = getApplicationContext().getDataDir().
getAbsolutePath();

try {
    Runtime.getRuntime().exec("touch "+filesLocation+"/test.
txt");
} catch (IOException e) {
    e.printStackTrace();
}
```

## CHAPTER 12

Decompiling and Disassembling Android Applications

Android applications are written in either Java or Kotlin. When an application is built, these are compiled down into Dalvik bytecode - represented in dex (Dalvik executable) files. This Dalvik bytecode is in binary, and so isn't human readable. This being the case, if a reverse engineer is looking to analyze an already-compiled Android application, they are left with the option to decompile or disassemble the Dalvik executable. The process of creating and reverse engineering an Android application is highlighted in Figure 12-1.

© James Stevenson 2021
J. Stevenson, *Android Software Internals Quick Reference*,
https://doi.org/10.1007/978-1-4842-6914-5_12

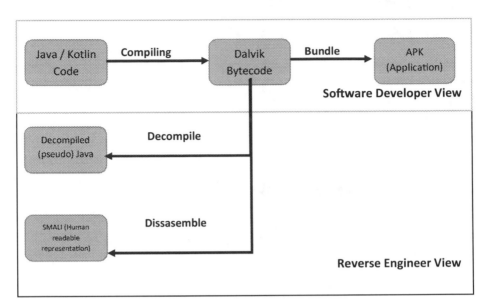

Figure 12-1. Software developer and reverse engineer process view

Decompiled Java

The first option is to use a tool to decompile the Dalvik bytecode to human-readable Java. This Java is more pseudocode than actual Java, as it's the decompiler's "best guess" at what the Dalvik assembly represents. While this view will be more familiar to Java developers, it normally isn't the best option, as not only is it not representative of the actual application code but it is also not runnable or recompilable. Tools such as dex2jar and jadx can be used for decompiling Dalvik executables. Jadx can be used to export a Jadx project to a Gradle project, in turn allowing for the project to be loaded into Android Studio.

APKTool can be used for extracting the .dex file from an APK:

```
apktool  -s d <apk path>
```

Decompile and view an APK or Dex file's decompiled java with JADX:

```
jadx -e <apk or dex file path>
```

Disassembled Dalvik Bytecode (Smali)

Instead of decompiling to pseudo-Java, a disassembler can be used to revert the Dalvik bytecode to a human-readable representation of itself. The more commonly used form of this for Dalvik bytecode is called Smali. The benefit of disassembling to Smali is that a dex file can be disassembled, read, modified, reassembled, and resigned and will still be in a fully functioning state.

Tools such as APKTool can be used to disassemble dalvik bytecode:

```
apktool d <path>
```

Due to its nature, Smali has a significantly larger code footprint than Java or Kotlin. For example, the following Toast code (a simple Android pop-up message) in Java is half the size of the same code in Smali.

Java:

```
Context context = getApplicationContext();
CharSequence text = "I'm a Toast";
int duration = Toast.LENGTH_SHORT;

Toast toast = Toast.makeText(context, text, duration);
toast.show();
```

Smali:

```
.line 13
const-string v0, "I'm a Toast!"

.line 14
.local v0, "text":Ljava/lang/String;
const/4 v1, 0x1

.line 16
.local v1, "duration":I
invoke-virtual {p0}, Lcom/example/simpletoastapp/MainActivity;-
>getApplicationContext()Landroid/content/Context;

move-result-object v2

move-object v3, v0

check-cast v3, Ljava/lang/CharSequence;

invoke-static {v2, v3, v1}, Landroid/widget/Toast;-
>makeText(Landroid/content/Context;Ljava/lang/CharSequence;I)
Landroid/widget/Toast;

move-result-object v2

.line 17
.local v2, "toast":Landroid/widget/Toast;
invoke-virtual {v2}, Landroid/widget/Toast;->show()V
```

Extracting APKs from Running Devices

In order to analyze (and in turn disassemble or decompile) an Android application, you may need to first extract it from a device. The ADB shell can be used to do this.

The following uses the package manager to list all package IDs on the device:

```
pm list packages
pm list packages | grep chrome
```

Next, package manager can be used again to list the path to the base APK of the desired package (an example package path is /data/app/ com.android.chrome-6piH3g1ET8uQozATuKwptQ==/base.apk):

```
pm path <Package ID>
```

No special permissions are required to view the directories returned by this command. However, its parent directory (`/data/app`) does not have read permissions for nonroot, meaning that applications on the device cannot be enumerated in this way.

Finally, the simplest way to extract the APK is by using adb with the following:

```
adb pull <package base APK path>
```

It is also worth bearing in mind that tools such as APK Hoarder,[1] which is free and open source, can be used for the mass extraction of APKs from a device.

---

[1]"APK Hoarder | Github" `https://github.com/user1342/APK-Hoarder`. Accessed 27 Dec. 2020.

CHAPTER 13

Closing Thoughts

The purpose of this book has been to supply you with a reference guide on information useful to Android software developers working closely with the Android OS and other Android security elements. This book has covered areas from application sandboxing and the Dalvik Virtual Machine to storage types for Android applications and how to reverse engineer an already-compiled Android application.

It's important to bear in mind that while the core principles in this book should continue to be relevant for many years to come, some aspects may change as new versions of Android are released. This being the case, while continuing to use this book as a reference guide, also review the footnotes scattered throughout the book to build upon the covered areas.

There are a plethora of other amazing resources out there to support your knowledge in Android programming, internals, and reverse engineering; a selection of these has been included here:

- **Maddie Stone** - Android App Reverse Engineering 101[1]

- **Jonathan Levin** - Android Internals[2]

---

[1]"Android App Reverse Engineering 101 | Ragingrock" https://ragingrock.com/AndroidAppRE/ Accessed 27 Dec. 2020.

[2]"Android Internals| NewAndroidBook " http://newandroidbook.com/ Accessed 27 Dec. 2020.

- **Kristina Balaam** - Android Malware Analysis |
  YouTube[3]

- **Kristina Balaam** - Android Malware Analysis |
  LinkedIn Learning[4]

- **Ira R. Forman and Nate Forman** - Java Reflection in
  Action | Manning[5]

- **Android Documentation** | Android Developers[6]

In addition to these resources, I'd also like to give a special mention to JD, a fellow researcher and software engineer in the field, without whom I wouldn't have been encouraged to write this book.

For more information on and more resources from me, the author of this book, James Stevenson, please visit my website at `https://JamesStevenson.me/`.

---

[3]"Android Malware Analysis | YouTube" `https://www.youtube.com/channel/UCRHFnRniDEGJCZgsEgtUPxA` Accessed 27 Dec. 2020.

[4]"Android Malware Analysis | LinkedIn Learning" `https://www.lynda.com/Android-tutorials/Learning-Android-Malware-Analysis/2812563-2.html` Accessed 27 Dec. 2020.

[5]Java Reflection in Action | Manning" `https://www.manning.com/books/java-reflection-in-action` Accessed 01 Jan. 2021.

[6]Android Documentation | Android Developer" `https://developer.android.com/` Accessed 27 Dec. 2020.

Index

A

Activity class, 8
Activity context, 22, 23
Activity life cycle
  onCreate(), 24
  onPause(), 25
  onRestart(), 25
  onResume(), 24
  onStart(), 24
  onStop(), 25
adb logcat command, 91
ADB shell, 157
AES encryption, 102–104
AlarmManager, 108
Android application activity life
  cycle, 24
Android Debug Bridge (adb), 3
Android ID, 87
Android Launcher
  application creation, 130
  functionality, 131–133
  settings, 129
AndroidManifest.xml package
  attribute, 53
Android permissions, 15–18, 20, 21

Android Runtime (ART), 7
Android Sandbox, 7, 8
Android Shell, 147–151
Android users, 27, 28
Android versions, 4, 5
Application components
  broadcast receivers, 8
  content providers, 9
  manifest file, 9, 10
Application context, 22, 23
Application ID
  build.gradle file, 55
  Gradle build file, 56
Application ID, 52
  Google Play Store listing, 55
  internal storage file path, 55
  rules, 55
  suffix and flavor, 57
Application's manifest file, 9, 10
Assets folder, 81, 83
AsyncTask, 105
  battery and security effects
    app standby buckets,
      124, 125
    doze, 123, 124
  types, 121

Printed in the United States
by Baker & Taylor Publisher Services